A CHILD IS
BEING KILLED

M E R I D I A N

Crossing Aesthetics

Werner Hamacher

& David E. Wellbery

Editors

Translated by
Marie-Claude Hays

Stanford
University
Press

Stanford
California
1998

A CHILD IS
BEING KILLED

*On Primary Narcissism and
the Death Drive*

Serge Leclaire

A Child Is Being Killed
was originally published in French in 1975 as
*On tue un enfant: Un essai sur le narcissisme
primaire et la pulsion de mort*
© 1975 Editions du Seuil

Assistance for this translation was provided by
the French Ministry of Culture

Stanford University Press
Stanford, California

Printed in the United States of America

CIP data appear at the end of the book

Contents

A CHILD IS
BEING KILLED

§ 1 Pierre-Marie,
or the Child

Why was it put up there, atop the monumental fireplace? It fell on the stone floor, in front of the hearth. Luckily, it's only the child of the Virgin, a wonderful Romanesque statue. She was presenting the child, standing erect in front of her. He's broken: his head is still attached to his left shoulder, his feet are cut off and his trunk split apart, but his legs and thighs are intact to just above his genitals. Can he be put back together again? It's nothing: the trunk isn't shattered, in fact it's almost in one piece, I'm sure. In one piece. But he's not moving. Mommy! It's my child alright, already cold in front of the fire, which has flared up again. This can't be. And yet I want to cry out. I spring up screaming. I can't hear anything and I rush over, convinced he has fallen from the dresser where I put him down while getting his nightclothes. How did I fall asleep in this armchair? Or is it he who fell while sleeping? I want someone to come and tear me away from this memory. Did I scream or did he? I want to sleep, to forget everything. No, I want to wake up, to finally wake up. All I can be sure of is the fire. Could I be dead? Yes. I'm the one who is dead. . . . If only I had never been born!

The entire space has vanished, between the glory of the infant-king and the sorrow of the Pietà. There is no longer any difference between the Sacred Story and what I can't stop being unable to live.

"Father, can't you see I'm burning?" dreams the man who, for a few hours, has given up watching over his dead child. "Father, can't you see the Erl-King?" says the clear-sighted child to his father, who is taking him away on a wild ride. "Can't you hear the sweet promises of the Erl-King?" "No, it's nothing. Be at peace, my son. It's mist drifting by, the wind murmuring in the dead leaves."

Can't you see, can't you hear? No, it can't be. A child's death is unbearable: it fulfills our most secret and profound wishes. One can conceive of a neighbor's death without excessive grief. Indeed, one might agree, with or without debate, to killing or even eating him. The horror of parricide seems to be getting more familiar: once a sacred tragedy, Oedipus has now become a complex. The right is granted, at least to the imagination, to tear one's mother to pieces and to kill one's father. (The trouble is, says the good doctor, you haven't killed off your father yet!) But killing a child? No! We rediscover the sacred horror. It just can't be. God himself stops the hand of Abraham: the sacrifice will be carried out, but with a lamb in the place of Isaac. The infant-king, the "Son of God," must be marked with the grace of having escaped the massacre of the first-born so that, when he reaches manhood, the mystery of death and redemption can take place. We were already in the Story, and we are not out of it yet.

From where the analyst is sitting, what is at stake is the truth. There is no way out: reckoning with the absolute power of the *in-fans*, he must never stop perpetrating the murder of the child, even as he recognizes that he cannot carry it out. Psychoanalytic practice is based upon bringing to the fore *the constant work of a power of death—the death of the wonderful (or terrifying) child who, from generation to generation, bears witness to parents' dreams and desires. There can be no life without killing that strange, original image in which everyone's birth is inscribed.* It is an impossible but necessary murder, for there can be no life, no life of desire and creation, if we ever stop killing off the always returning "wonderful child."

The wonderful child is first of all the nostalgic gaze of the mother who made him into an object of extreme magnificence akin to the Child Jesus majesty, a light and jewel radiating forth absolute power. But he is already the forsaken one as well, lost in total dereliction, facing terror and death alone. In the extraordinary presence of the child in the flesh, the radiant image of the infant-king, stronger even than his cries or laughter and counterbalanced by the sorrow of the Pietà, compels attention. Through him shines the royal figure of our wishes, memories, hopes, and dreams—a fragile and hieratic figure *representing*, in the secret theater where destiny is played out, the first- (or third-) person position from which the unconscious speaks. For each of us, the wonderful child is the unconscious, primordial representation in which, more densely than anywhere else, our wishes, nostalgia, and hopes come together. In the transparent reality of the child, the Real of all our desires can be seen, almost without a veil. We are fascinated and can neither look away nor grasp it.

To give it up is to die, to no longer have a reason for living. But to pretend that we can hold on to it is to condemn ourselves not to live. There is for everyone, always, a child to kill. The loss of a representation of fullness, of motionless *jouissance*, must be relentlessly mourned and mourned. A light must be eclipsed so it can shine and spread out on a background of darkness. Whoever does not mourn, over and over, the loss of the wonderful child he might have been remains in limbo—in the milky light of a shadowless, hopeless waiting. But whoever believes he has won the battle against the figure of the tyrant once and for all cuts himself off from the sources of his creative spirit and thinks he is strong when he stubbornly resists the reign of *jouissance*.

This is a common enough fate, which can lead its victim either to slumber in the fashionable hedonism of the day or else to pretend to awaken and imagine a world he will dream grandiosely of putting into order for the good of all, his omnipotence having crept back through the window of his anguish (which he thought was closed). Must we, then, to defend ourselves against the fascination of the wonderful child, accept like Abraham the sacrifice of our child; order, like Pharaoh and Herod, the killing of all the firstborn; offer up our child to God, tyrant, or country? Must we devote ourselves to some "cause" that will survive us, or more simply to a woman, a man, or children?

Any domestic "order" or, even more so, any social order will presume to account for this elusive or lost image of happiness and downfall, glory and impotence. But in fact all it does is distract us. For no "order" can spare us from our own death, not the one that is ritualized in wars and religions but rather our *first death*, the one we must go through from the very moment of our birth—the one we know and never cease to talk about, since every day we have to live through the death of the wonderful or terrifying child in the dreams of those who bore us or witnessed our birth. Killing one's parents is not enough, not by a long shot. The point is to kill the tyrannical representation of His Majesty the Baby: "I" begin at that moment, already subjected to the inexorable second death—the other, about which nothing can be said.

It is common practice to confuse the "first death," the one we must continually live through, with the "second death." This is a stubborn and solidly anchored confusion: not only does it allow us to not recognize the most imperative summons of our bondage— to be born again and again to language and desire, all the while never ceasing to mourn the loss of the fascinating *infans*—but it also gives us the illusion of working against death, no matter how doomed the endeavor. The results of this confusion give a measure of how deeply rooted it is: the glorification of failure or the making of life into a sacred venture, the cult of despair or the defense of faith. Here is a brief example. The logic behind suicide derives from a perfect syllogism: in order to live, I must kill "myself"; or else, I don't really feel alive (this is no life!), therefore I commit suicide. If only we could clear up (*but at the cost of what labor?*) the confusion underlying the truth of the first statement—in order to live I must kill the tyrannical representation of the *infans* within me—then another logic would appear. This new logic would be governed by the impossibility of ever carrying out this murder once and for all and by the need to commit it every time we start to truly speak, and every moment that we begin to love.

∼

The price can be high, at times.

Witness the experience of certain of my partners in the passion of psychoanalysis for whom work left unfinished led to tragedy. To sit behind the couch and listen to analysands brings into play and puts to the test one's own relationship to the *primary narcissistic representation* I have so far been calling the wonderful child. It brings into play, without ever making a show of it, the strangely familiar representation that makes us up—the *infans* in us. It puts to the test the constancy of the power of death that keeps us open to the voice of desire. Probably for want of plainly stating the difference between the two deaths each of us experiences and of making it clear that the foundation of our analytic work is always to recognize the true object of the power of death, I allowed the "unconscious" work of my analyst-analysands—who were more determined than they realized to see it all the way through—to be carried out, with fatal results for their own children: some were stillborn, premature, deformed; some were suddenly and inexplicably taken gravely ill in their early years; others, still, had near-suicidal accidents. When death or harm actually befalls a child, then the power of death at work in analysis is dramatically demonstrated. The killing of the primary narcissistic representation implied in analytic work is expressed in reality for having failed to clear up the common confusion between the true work of death to which we are subjected, and organic death, which can be conceived, by anyone who speaks and desires, only in reference to the first—obliteration or resurrection. Let me add that in other cases, I can be blamed for a different outcome, as when the attention to the necessary killing of the primary narcissistic representation implied by psychoanalytic work had the opposite effect: whether the analytic passion of the analyst-analysand was less intense or whether I was simply an inadequate listener, he or she went from believing that they were sterile to making babies.

I have brought up these extreme cases only because they force us to consider the absolutely compelling power of the most "primal" of all phantasies:[1] "a child is being killed." That it surfaces in psychoanalytic work, most often in a disguised form, is of course the rule. But it is remarkable that, until now, emphasis has been laid on its satellites in the oedipal constellation—phantasies of murdering the father, of sleeping with the mother or tearing her to pieces. No account is taken of the attempt to kill Oedipus the child, although the failure of that attempt is what settled the hero's tragic fate.

The phantasy "a child is being beaten," which seems benign enough even if it cannot be expressed without some reticence, readily reaches consciousness. On the other hand, except for the likes of Gilles de Rais, "a child is being killed" appears as a phantasy, as a structure of desire, only in the course of psychoanalytic work.

So, for example, an analysand we will call Renaud often replays in wakeful fantasy a childhood dream that resists the work of analysis because it just seems too simple. It consists of a very brief scene. In a drawing room, his father is attacked by an intruder who, without warning, shoots him in the belly; although he tries to avoid the bullets by jumping, legs apart, he is hit and falls flat on the ground, face down. It's clear: the father is murdered by the dreamer's proxy, the intruder. What makes this interpretation inadequate is not its psychoanalytically orthodox simplicity. Rather, it is the fact that, on the one hand, the daydream gets repeated and, on the other, the symptom that triggered the recollection of the dream persists—a painful sensitivity in the left pelvic cavity, a pain described as an internal bruise and that returns with the least provocation. The dream must therefore be analyzed in all its details. First of all, the avoidance action—jumping up, legs apart. This gesture conjures up a scene in which the father is chasing a bully who had attacked little Renaud and was about to do him in. It is unclear whether the attacker was actually cornered in a spectacular pursuit, but there is a definite picture of someone (the dreamer as a child? a man?) trying to block his flight by spreading out his arms and legs.

The fight provoking this vengeful pursuit forces on Renaud another story, taking the place of a memory, of a violent argument with his older brother. The nature of the confrontation is unclear. Could it be that Renaud, the youngest, had the upper hand thanks to the energetic blow of a hammer on his dear brother's head? Or was it the other way around? Two features remain constant in the midst of these doubts—a solid fratricidal hate and the deep-down sense of always having within himself some hidden resource enabling him, under all circumstances, to be the strongest. It would be tedious to enumerate the details associated with "in the belly"; but they lead, as one might expect, to a series of childish confusions that have come up earlier in the analysis—that babies are conceived orally, anally, and through the navel—and to a profound hostility toward the mother, crystallized around a quite common anal persecution. What's more, his mother had twice undergone surgery "in the belly." His memory of her second operation, for an intestinal occlusion, is perfectly detailed, but the first one has remained mysterious. It was most likely gynecological in nature and probably caused sterility, but he can't help suspecting that it was for a miscarriage, although this suspicion can neither be ruled out nor confirmed. In both cases, it seems that the mother almost died. His heartrending effusions over each convalescence bear witness to Renaud's "ambivalent" feelings. Beyond the "killing of the father," we had everything we needed to recognize his feelings toward his mother—passionate love and the phantasy of tearing her to pieces. But even after it was elucidated, the initial daydream kept recurring, always enigmatically, and the symptom persisted. We had to get back to the mangled child, the one who appeared clearly in the first memory and was confirmed by at least two others. In one, a helpless Renaud is attacked, at the corner of a square, by someone stronger. In the other, Renaud does in one of his faithful friends who had been getting on his nerves more than usual. I could go on unwinding the thread of associations—the dead mother of another close friend, a beloved neighbor and friend marked by a birth trauma.

Slowly, the "archaic" logic of the unconscious takes hold: just as the mother, who is in a position of power, appears to have a penis, the father, in a protective position, can appear to be *big with child*.

This is a secret phantasy quite familiar to analysts. What is being hit and killed in the paternal figure in the dream is probably Renaud himself, who acknowledges feeling that he is, above all, his father's son. From then on, it is his own image as a wonderful and prodigious child—like so many children—that comes to the fore on the stage of his unconscious. Something changes for him . . . to be continued and taken up later.

This example shows that the elements of the original phantasy that "a child is being killed" do not lend themselves to being heard early on. Too often, the initial satisfaction derived from elucidating a fragment of unconscious desire stops our work and leaves the essential part of analysis undone.

At this point, we can probably postulate, without getting ahead of ourselves or extrapolating, that the repetition of the memory (phantasy, dream) and the resistance of the symptom make it imperative to pursue the work of analysis beyond the satisfaction of early recognition. We can also say that the representation of a mangled child, even if it is veiled, disguised, or displaced, is to be taken as a clue not to be overlooked. Even a little drowned cat and a puppy run over by a car are not to be dismissed. The violent turmoil triggered, even in the guise of irony or humor, by their evocation—or their current repetition—must be heard in order to let unfold the absolutely constraining power of the necessary death in each of us.

This is how, in the story of Pierre-Marie, the repetitive insistence and emotional charge accompanying his memory of a puppy being drowned by his father led us back to the death of an older brother, not yet a year old, whose name was also Pierre. After our preliminary meetings, there had been no further mention of this crucial event in his prehistory. Pierre-Marie figures as a replacement for Pierre, and his problem consists entirely in killing off the representation "Pierre-Marie" as the living substitute for his dead brother. Suffice it to say for now that the violence of his rage toward his father killing the little dog and his great compassion for the animal brought us to the dead end, which was decisive for

Pierre-Marie, of baby Pierre's death. From that moment on in his analysis, he would dream of wandering through cemeteries, phantasize his father's death, wish for his mother's death and, while he was at it, his wife's. He started arguing violently with his eldest daughter, to the point of sending her into . . . analysis. Although the dead child had appeared in his analysis, he remained something of a dead letter, and we were very far from being able to consider the fact that the child to kill was Pierre-Marie himself. Nevertheless, it was already possible to recognize the gaps in meaning characteristic of the grammatical structure of phantasy: thus, in the place of "the child" being killed, came the puppy, father, mother, wife, his own child. The indefinite way in which the phantasy "a child is being killed" is formulated is perfectly fitting: only the verb is precise, indicating the act of killing, of putting to death. We don't know who is killing nor what "child" is being killed. We need only mention the possible variations on the killer's identity: the father, where the puppy is concerned (but who or what is responsible for Pierre's death?), the doctor (suggestive of the analyst), the too negligent or passionate mother, destiny, age, or even himself? The series of figures that could occupy the place of the agent is limitless. Never mind! If we bear in mind the resoluteness of the action in the phantasy, killing, and the relative specificity of the object, the child, we notice that what is essential in the phantasy is its grammatical structure.

I will therefore address the phantasy's fundamental question: *what child?* In the case of Pierre-Marie, it will become apparent that the child to be killed is none other than Pierre-Marie, and we shall see what makes this particular putting-to-death so very difficult. We are not going to follow our patient blindly in his suicidal phantasies, in which he takes to imagining that what is at stake is the death of the calm and collected man he appears to be. The Pierre-Marie to be killed is *the representation of his mother's desire*, a representation so aptly named Pierre-Marie, after his dead brother and the Virgin-mother. What has to be killed so that Pierre-Marie can live is the representation so closely tied to his name and which first appears as that of a consoling child: the dead child's living substitute, destined to be immortal, the unstated figure of his mother's wishes. What is to be killed is a representation presiding, like a star, over the destiny of the child in the flesh. This "heavenly sign," the primary signifier determining the mother's desire, is not often as easy to identify as it is in Pierre-Marie's story. It is a properly speaking unconscious representation, all the more difficult (if not impossible) to locate and to name in that it is inscribed in one, two, or many others' unconscious, which is to say in the desire of those who gave birth to the child or witnessed his birth.

Here three points should be stressed. First of all, the status and the always problematical identification of the unconscious representation of the parents' desire—in this case, Pierre-Marie as consolation and living substitute for a dead child—are profoundly different from the possibilities of identification or constitution of Pierre-Marie as subject. Furthermore, Pierre-Marie's unconscious subject, that is to say his own unconscious representatives, will inescapably take shape largely in relation to his mother's unconscious representation. Lastly, the unconscious representative of the mother's phantasy, regardless of how it is specifically represented or signified (e.g., a devouring rather than consoling child, or Pierre as a heart of stone),[2] will be cathected by the subject's unconscious as a privileged representative, the strangest, most intimate and disquieting of all. It will be cathected as a representative that never has been and never will be his own, yet whose absolute strangeness will form what in him is most secret, indeed sacred (which we could understand, without any negative connotations, as abject). This privileged unconscious representative is what I call the *primary narcissistic representative. The child to be killed*, the child to be glorified, the all-powerful, terrifying child, is *the representation of the primary narcissistic representative.* Accursed and universally shared, it is part of everyone's inheritance: the object of a murder as imperative as it is impossible.

The primary narcissistic representation fully deserves to be called *infans.* It does not and never will speak. Precisely to the extent that one begins to kill it can one begin to speak. To the extent that one goes on killing it can one go on truly to speak, and to desire.

Pierre-Marie lives painfully and laboriously, haunted by the paralyzing presence of death. He partakes only fitfully in the joys of his family, limiting his passions and desire to their pale shadow. Most of his energy is devoted to this kind of stifling activity and only bears fruits—which he can't enjoy—in his professional endeavors. What he demands is to be delivered from this fear of death. The provisional identification of this death as Pierre's builds a solid bridgehead in the retrenchment of his defenses. What he is looking for in dreams where he jumps over walls, digs trenches, and discovers tombs in abandoned cemeteries is his brother. He wants to finally get even with the little creep. But how do you kill the dead? As an answer, Pierre-Marie can look at himself, a child vowed immortal by his mother even before he was born, in the place of his dead brother. He burns like a mortuary lamp destined never to go out. And yet, if he wishes to live, he must let that image of light go out and once more kill his brother, thereby wreaking havoc with his mother's dream, doing in the immortal child of her desire: he must kill the very representative he has himself enshrined as the core, however foreign, of his own being in order to make of it his "primary narcissistic representative," Pierre-Marie-the-perfect-child. He is a good and loving son to his aging parents, attentive to their every need, just as he is a good father. A first child, unwanted or so he believes, forced him into a marriage he constantly questions, without yet realizing that having children is a way of getting himself off the hook and an attempt to come out of limbo. How can he kill the child of light he is for his mother? Will he succeed before he buries his parents? Help me, he says, as if he wanted me to guide his penis in the ways of desire. What he is really asking me to do is to raise the sacrificial knife and slay him like the beast in the ritual, so that he can be reborn from the ashes or blood of the double-headed tyrant, dead-Pierre-to-be-killed and Pierre-Marie-the-memorial-to-be-destroyed. This first death could then finally lead him into an interval between deaths, where he can live.

What makes living so very hard for Pierre-Marie is thus tied to the fact that by questioning his primary narcissistic representation he touches his mother to the quick of her unconscious. In his mother's wish, he must be and remain the immortal child who replaces Pierre and cancels out his death. But by renouncing his identification with the image of the luminous child built around his mother's dream, Pierre-Marie deals her a fatal blow: not only does he destroy the keystone of the dream she lives by, he also kills Pierre a second time, thereby forcing her to go through the mourning she has never completed. This is quite a heavy task for a "good son," or so he persists in thinking. The work of analysis will have to elucidate and untie all the secondary elaborations that, in his life, have come to mask the necessity of killing the child (of the primary narcissistic representation), especially all that he has invested in his own children in the name of negating or realizing his own narcissistic death.

The case of Pierre-Marie outlines how difficult it is to name the primary narcissistic representative as a living commemorative child. It also illustrates the problem imposed on each of us by that phantasy, "a child is being killed." Even if there is no dead brother in the family story, the parents' desire is always marked by some unfinished act of mourning—if only for their own childhood dreams. Always and above all, their offspring will provide a fine foundation on which to invest what they had to renounce.

The primary narcissism of children . . . is less easy to grasp by direct observation than to confirm by inference from elsewhere. If we look at the attitude of affectionate parents towards their children, we have to recognize that it is a revival and reproduction of their own narcissism. . . . Thus they are under a compulsion to ascribe every perfection to the child. . . . The child shall have a better time than his parents; he shall not be subject to the necessities which they have recognized as paramount in life. Illness, death, renunciation of enjoyment, restrictions on his own will, shall not touch him; the laws of nature and of society shall be abrogated in his favour; he shall once more really be the center and core of creation—"His Majesty the Baby," as we once fancied ourselves. The child shall fulfill those wishful dreams of the parents which they never carried out—the boy shall become a great man and a hero in his father's place, and the girl shall marry a prince as a tardy compensation for her mother. At the most touchy point in the narcissistic system, the immortality of the ego, which is so hard pressed by reality, security is achieved by taking refuge in the child. Parental love, which is so moving and at bottom so childish, is nothing but the parents' narcissism born again.[3]

To undertake the "killing of the child" and sustain the necessary destruction of the primary narcissistic representation (primary narcissism in Freud's text) is everyone's task, as imperative as it is impossible to complete. How can the child be eliminated? How can one get rid of something unconscious, therefore indelible? Conversely, however, how can one avoid that necessity or elude that constraint without remaining in the limbo of the *infans,* on this side of desire? For such is indeed the "insane" destiny awaiting anyone who cannot begin to murder the all-powerful child and destroy the primary narcissistic representation. The primary narcissistic representation (the child in ourselves) is indelible, as is any unconscious representative; moreover, to call that representation unconscious—quite rightly—is to say that it does not nor did it ever present the least inroad to consciousness. How, therefore, can one conceive giving up something to which one has never had access? Such is the general problem attending our connection with unconscious representatives proper, those under the sway of original repression, which we can know only, if luxuriously, from its effects, in other words its offshoots.

We have only to recall the example analyzed by Freud, of his screen memory of picking buttercups and being interrupted by an afternoon snack. The true unconscious representatives—yellow (*Gelb*), loaf (*Laib*) of bread and its irreplaceable taste or smell (*Geschmack*), the body (*Leib*) of his cousin or maid—remain outside of any real grasp, especially for after-the-fact analytic investigation. Even in analytical work, unconscious representatives do not reveal themselves directly but only in their effects on the organization of the symptom or phantasy. An analytical process would have been needed for the ambiguity in "*Laib/Leib*" and the sensorial reference in *Gelb* and *Geschmack* to be sent back, or even decomposed, by an other in the position of analyst. Only then could it be determined, from the effect on the covering-up organization of the memory, whether those terms are truly fragments of unconscious representatives—which in no way means that such a localization of unconscious representatives erases their determining traces: in fact, an organization that is different from its effects is the hallmark of an exact localization.

So, for example, if we go back to Renaud, two elements of the dream seem to point to unconscious representatives: "jumping, legs apart" and "in the belly." Legs apart, in readiness to confront the adversary with exaltation and panic, braced with a keen sensation focusing on the genitals exposed in that position; a set of organic sensations confirmed by the movement of the jump, which puts the exaltation in motion while triggering the void of panic, and which in the dream ends with his falling flat on his face. Images of fragmentation, of legs cut off in a tramway accident, the phantasy of a torso separated from the pelvis, the image of quartering, of an impossible or catastrophic bridge while doing the splits, but especially a sensation of de-composition in front of a threat, a danger, an aggression experienced as a questioning of a very fragile and vivid feeling of narcissistic wholeness; it's an internal panic, betrayed by the decomposition of the face and opening onto the possibility of all kinds of violence. "In the belly" also speaks of this "viscerally" unconscious representation of panic and excess, this feeling of a place, of oneness and converging encounters, marked by the most extreme vulnerability; but he adds to it the specification of a place mysteriously giving rise to the Unknown, be it rare harmony or abject thing, shit or splendor. As Renaud's analysis progresses, starting with the screen-dream of the father's murder, there appear, through the images and words of the dream, fragments of unconscious representatives that one can provisionally call composition/decomposition, disarticulation, engendering; or describe in more pictorial terms, as the decomposition of a face through which can be seen the fragile and powerful picture of a quiet and violent hope: Renaud himself.

∽

To approach an unconscious representative is to recognize the range of representations it has engendered in a constraining way within their substitutive value and thereby to unveil something of its tyrannical power. To shed light on a few features of Renaud's darkened and decomposed face, to begin perceiving the marmoreal power of the immortal child in the figure of Pierre-Marie, is tantamount to demolishing the blindness of their power by recognizing them as unconscious representatives; it is the start of the undoing of destiny's most fascinating figure: the child in ourselves.

§ 2 Béatrice,
or Love

Whenever, in a moment of grace, it comes over to me to tell a woman "I love you," something in me bursts open, whereby I am reborn. This sense of wonder is triggered by her "beauty," made of a glow that bewitches me, a light in which I bathe and which gives every bit of her body, her smell, her voice, her skin, her words, an irrefutable attraction. I lose myself in her ear, mouth, hair, the small of her back, assured all at once of a reason for my torment or peace: she loves me and I am afraid, without believing it, that the moment of grace will vanish. No, she is waiting for me and I want her; we each have the absolute certainty, when we embrace, that together we have found the source of earth, water, and fire: it is a moment of truth well before death.

It may be prudent, if not wise, to say that truth is bound to remain hidden. What child is not truly a wonder, what spring not miraculous as it flows forth? If truth speaks, it is with the voice of the unconscious, and no better voice can say it, at the heart of what makes it speak, than the *jouissance* of lovers. Sitting back in his armchair, the analyst is listening for it. Yet in no other place than that of love can one meet the figure of the golden number that orders the truth of the unconscious, pressing its seal on each of the representations that make it up. Its name is *phallus*. The power of the child cannot adequately represent it nor can the beauty of the woman or the presumptuous challenge of the erect penis. If they each glow with truth, it is because their blossoming takes root directly in the unconscious, and their exposed glory conceals the immediacy of the figure that no writing can trace without altering it.

More inconceivable still than an unconscious representative, the phallus, with its intrinsically heterogeneous formal structure, is nothing but lack and source. Even the concept of the penis cannot be defined simply as a part of the body. It cannot be conceived solely in terms of the different organizations of which it partakes, the physiological body and the body of *jouissance*, whose functioning and logic are absolutely distinct. The fact that the penis is both difference and sign of difference, both the sexual organ and the visible sign of the difference between the sexes, must be taken into account. Lastly, the most important fact that must be taken into account is that the relation of which the penis is one of the agents cannot in any way be formalized without reducing it to reproductive copulation, to the extent that the *jouissance* encountered comes within no other order than that of the unconscious. The phallus, therefore, as a referent of the unconscious order, cannot be grasped as a concept: like a prime number proposing the impossible, its division, it escapes all inscriptions through the cut in its unity. There is no text or image of the phallus: it can be encountered only through the *jouissance* of bodies, in the risk of love. Its only concept is unconscious: castration.

"Unconscious," for it is in the unconscious that the workings of "a little something separable from the body" operate; "concept," since the term escapes Freud when he writes about it.[1] In the primary sense of the term, *castration* designates, through the conscious representations of loss of the penis, a double process. On the one hand, the phallus differs from the unconscious representative while imprinting it with its seal of intrinsic heterogeneity. On the other hand, the relation between conscious and unconscious representation is outlined as an irreversible engendering process.

Let's take, for example, a common symptom of the phobia of closed spaces. It is not enough to link the representation of the

closed space to a general form of unconscious representation, that
of the disquieting space of the maternal body. However relevant
the interpretative construction connecting the anxiety-producing
closed space with the unconscious, phantasmic representation of
the "inside" of the mother's body may be, the symptom will persist, for it has nowhere to go. It is impossible for the conscious representation to return to the unconscious. The analytical work
called for must focus on the organization of the unconscious representation that produced the symptom. Is the unconsciously
phantasized interior of the maternal body laid out like a labyrinth,
tunnel, waterfall, or cave, as in romantic voyages "to the center of
the earth," or, on the contrary, like a vast empty dome? Do you fall
into it through a crevice opening up under your feet or are you
sucked in through a menacing mouth? Does it offer the shelter of
a sweet, paradise-like climate or leave you exposed to hungry, terrifying monsters? Only through truly analytical work addressing
the singular strangeness of the unconscious representation of
closed spaces can one hope to remove the anxiety tied to it. The
concept of castration refers first and foremost to the irreparable
break that makes for no going back on the one-way path between
the unconscious representations and their offshoots, the conscious
representations.

To limit it to that sense, however, would be to singularly reduce
its range of meaning. The concept of castration designates above
all the operation through which the unconscious representation,
"inside the mother's body," is both constituted as "sexual" by taking on the phallic stamp, the primary model of the sexual break,
and differentiated from the heterogeneity of the phallic referent.
The unconscious representative bears the phallic stamp in that it
proves to be a *signifier of jouissance*. But as such, it is only one of
the means of *jouissance* and leaves the other term unaccounted for,
the *object* without sign or image but which is nonetheless primordial. In that sense, the unconscious representative stands apart
from the phallus, both signifier and object of *jouissance*. *Castration*
essentially designates *the separation of the functional unit* in the unconscious system (*the unconscious representative*, or signifier in a La-

canian sense) *from the phallus*, which can only be referred to, contradictorily, as a signifier without a text and an object without an image, *a heterogeneous referent, shying away from any assigned place* in the order of *jouissance*.

Jouissance is the experience of the connection to the phallus, the meeting with the referent from the unconscious order, which is reached by each of us, man or woman, only through the other. It is where the space of love opens up. Orgasm bears witness to the extra-ordinariness of this meeting, even if the truth it imposes is commonly misunderstood: what characterizes it is the mobilization and release of a flow of energy, properly speaking *jouissance*. Orgasm has nothing in common with the partial experiences that bring into play a limited quantity of energy while producing *pleasure* focused on a part of the body. For in "true" love, the meeting with the phallus reveals the extra-ordinariness of the unconscious order's field of forces; it is a field ordered around the already split phallic nucleus, and its formidable power cannot be recognized according to the common measure or reason familiar to us in the conscious order and its reasonable economy.

Whereas the phallus is encountered only in love, in psychic life the elaboration of the connection to castration is ongoing: it determines the true sexual position of the subject, since castration cannot be reduced solely to anatomical facts. And yet, anatomy proves to be a determining factor, in that it intervenes in the process that organizes in different ways for men and women their relation to castration, defined as the overall set of operations making the unconscious representative, or signifier, into the functional unit in the unconscious system.

Here let us go back to the most exemplary of the unconscious representations, the primary narcissistic representation. We can now probably formulate more clearly what is meant by letting go of that representation: it consists in taking the process of castration into account. Again, it is a two-pronged process. On the one hand, it ensures the loss of the wonderful child: the splitting it creates gives him his status as a radically "repressed" unconscious representative of what is ordered as conscious system. On the other hand, in order to make the representation into a functional unit of the unconscious system, the castration process distinguishes it from the heterogeneous quality that weakens the phallic referent while marking it with its seal. The primary narcissistic representation of the wonderful child gets its fascinating power from its eminent value as a representative of the phallus, which can be found in the most conscious of formulations: the mother's meat and father's blood, flesh of their flesh and so completely different, signifier and product of their desires.

Assuming this, let us repeat that the experience of "loss" of the primary narcissistic representation, as of any unconscious representation, is inscribed in quite different ways according to anatomical differences. No matter when a girl becomes aware of her sexual reality, she does so in terms of lacking a penis. Has it been lost, or is it going to grow like the one she attributes, counter to perception, to the mother? Sooner or later, she will have to face the fact of lacking the penis. If we consider, as we must, the never-completed "loss" of the primary narcissistic representation as constitutive of castration proper, we can say that realizing the lack of a penis, which characterizes the girl's gender, will be inscribed for her as confirmation of a necessary loss tied to taking her place in the conflictual space of the word where desire unfolds. It is a space determined by the irreducible opposition of the conscious system to the unconscious system. Furthermore, if we take into account the experiences that analysis has taught us to understand as the "loss" of the oral object at the time of weaning, and then of the anal object—experienced as letting go of a part of the body—we can see that the "phallic" phase of the girl is inscribed at the time of its decline in a homogeneous series of losses or separations or a lack, falling *naturally* into place as it were in the structure of the unconscious, a structure controlled by castration.

This arrangement of experience, conditioned by anatomical givens, leaves woman disposed to an unmediated relationship to the workings of castration. She therefore finds herself on the same level with the process of original repression and invests little in the process of secondary repression (repression proper). The consciously rejected representations constituting the repressed of the "secondary" unconscious count less for her than the representatives of the "primary" unconscious (that of original repression). More precisely, all her experience confirms her—if she does not inopportunely deny it—in an acknowledgment of the "loss," that is to say of the determining primacy of the unconscious representation in the face of which the prestige of the conscious representation pales along with the conceptual apparatus it produces. For the woman, not only do words, above and beyond their signifying function, keep their value as unconscious representatives, as signifiers of *jouissance*, which will constitute her *woman's word*. In the immediacy of her connection to castration, she also finds support for a process of properly sexual identification that first and unconsciously specifies her as woman before any secondary identification of a trait or figure as belonging *to* womanhood.

On the contrary, for the man the experience of the phallic phase and its decline provides a break in the homogeneity of the series of losses: it is easy for him, confident in his possession of the penis, to fool himself and be persuaded that the phallus is not lost to everyone and that he, like all men, possesses it. The effect of this inevitable confusion is simple: it will intensify and confirm the secondary repression through which the truth of castration, as attested by unconscious representatives, will be more firmly denied and will furthermore ward off the infantile fear of losing the penis. *The man's discourse*, thus constituted as a discourse of secondary repression (in the common sense of the word) is clearly ordered then as the refusal of castration and misrecognition of the unconscious and therefore as a mode of exile from *jouissance*. Whatever the facts, confident in the tenacious illusion of not being castrated and of being in some way, since he has a penis, the possessor of the phallus, the man will insist on the primacy of conscious representations and the signifying values of words. He will elaborate conceptual systems with the ineradicable pretension of producing a universal discourse whose only function, in fact, is to occult the truth of unconscious discourse and the immovable radicalness of castration. Only repeated collisions against the "rock of castration" will force him to look back and question the reality he constructed for himself, to try and regain the real ground from which he is exiled. Rather than his mother or his origin, he rediscovers his mother tongue, articulated "in the name of the father," and at last treads upon his native soil, where the phallus lies keenly alive and unattached. The protest of women when they denounce the hegemonic tendency of the repressive function of man's discourse is not without foundation. But while it is without a doubt a discourse of repression and power, it is also absolutely the opposite of a properly labeled phallocentric discourse, which could only be a recognition of castration.

So, alongside an obvious anatomical determination, sexual identity is characterized as *a mode of entry in discourse*, as a radical subject position elaborated on the basis of the structural heterogeneity of the phallus. His body furnished with a penis, an objective guarantor of the signifying unity of the phallus, a man will situate his "I" in the break separating the conscious representation from the unconscious representative. This position lets go of the other part of the phallus, the object-related part, lacking as it does any assignable position. Of the unconscious concept of castration, the masculine position, which never stops elaborating itself in this way, retains only the break between conscious representation and unconscious representative and therefore takes no account of the split between the phallus and the unconscious representative—a split erased by the simplifying hypothesis of a structural identity between the two terms conceived as signifiers. The effect of this masculine position is to sustain the reality of castration by overinvesting in the conscious representation, safely cut off from the unconscious representation that engendered it, and therefore privileging the conscious rationality supporting it. Masculine destiny will remain stamped by the absolutely binding mortgage of its simplifying hypothesis, and a man will have no rest until he once again finds, through and in spite of all the ruses of his reason, the other half of the truth of the phallus, its intrinsic lack, and realizes castration.

Nothing predisposes the woman to reduce the phallus to a pure

signifier. Her privileged investment in the unconscious representative is a recognition of the distinctive split between the functional
unit of the unconscious and the phallus, object and cause of *jouissance.* The "I" spoken by a woman's voice locates itself between the
phallus and the functional unit of the unconscious representative.
But through this subject position, the woman tends to play down
the difference between the systems and to give importance, in the
conscious order, to the signifying value of words and representations rather than to their signification. By the same token, this
confusion of the orders dulls the *jouissance* value of the signifier
and forces her to privilege the object-related function of the phallus as sole guarantor of *jouissance.* Such is feminine destiny: to
imagine *a* phallus, since a woman knows only too well the uncanniness and evanescence of *the* phallus.

What matters in this approach to sexual reality imposed by analytical work is that sexual determination is a fact of discourse, a
radical subject position. This fact reveals that no universal discourse can lay claim to legitimacy because no discourse is asexual.
The space of discourse, therefore, reveals itself to be separated into
two systems, masculine and feminine, whose differentiation starts
with castration, in that castration organizes the connection to the
phallus around a half-truth. These discourses are stamped, at their
"origin," by the sexual split. It would be perfunctory to think they
could exist in a "pure state"; regardless of their respective dominance, their inevitable and necessary complexity constitutes what
has been perceived for a long time as "bisexuality." Let me add that
this complexity can go so far as to reverse for each of us the "natural" dominance of the discourse of our sex.

Jouissance, we were saying, is the experience of the connection to
the phallus, the meeting with the referent of the unconscious order
that can be reached, for man or woman, only through the other.

There is nothing in my beloved that does not move me uncon-
trollably. I feel transformed; each and every part of her gives me
the strange certainty of crossing my own borders. Nothing can replace her presence, and knowing that I can't stop wanting to tell

her "I love you" confirms my conviction that in her, through her, with her, a celebration of truth will be set ablaze. Her "beauty" is showing me the lights of the celebration to which we are invited, for she knows all its secrets far better than I do. I have to go back to the analyst's chair, the one where I sit and write, in order to reflect back, just as all my analysands do, on this experience of truth, and above all to stop ignoring it under the pretext that it would be difficult, or beneath his dignity, for an analyst to love. I must be able to write what loving means and what makes for its wonder, impasses, and failures.

Loving, for the man, means recognizing that a woman gives him access to primary castration, which differentiates the phallic referent from the unconscious representative and thereby unveils what cannot be looked at: the disabled phallus. To delight in her, through, with her, testifies to an encounter with the phallus that can take place in no other way than through love. Nothing can enable the man to cope with primary castration on his own, although he may have at his disposal a great many ways of fooling himself. Again, his handicap lies in the fact that he must necessarily misrecognize the defect of the phallus constituting him as a speaking and desiring subject. All he knows of the truth of castration is the difference between what is visible and invisible. Its other side stays hidden from him, however, the side making it possible to articulate the logic of the nonrepresentable, the difference between the invisible elements and the piercing/blinded eye that orders them like a vanishing point between the unconscious representatives and the phallus. Only when he is driven by a passion for clear-sightedness can a virile man be tempted to reconstruct that hypothetical other side, to glimpse the truth of the eye in the tomb, the final dazzling blindness of Oedipus, to laboriously articulate the proofs of the existence of the phallus. In search of castration without knowing it, he will become a "researcher," and sometimes an inventor, but, at that, only if he retains enough stamina to go beyond the seductive ruts lining the paths mapped out for gentlemen of good breeding: philosophy, scientific research, artistic creation, exploration, ethnology . . . psychoanalysis—or if he can retain some irony toward such perfectly virile activities as building families, fortunes, highways, dams (!), cities, companies, empires.

He needs a great deal of virtue not to be content with the legitimate satisfaction provided by these noble activities and to keep alive in him the drive to know the other side of truth, which can be reached neither alone nor through the shared illusion of a homosexual community or a sexless society. This presupposes a clear-sighted renunciation of faith in a phantasmic omnipotence surreptitiously present in the exercise of thought and the display of "creative" forces. Above all, it presupposes a heart open to the risk of loving without guarantee not to lose one's most glistening feathers by it, one's most solid assurances, even one's quality stamp of good breeding. Nothing can replace the knowledge of the phallus, which can be reached only through the experience of *jouissance*. The absolutely constraining way to it is through sex, with the woman he loves opening for him the space of that other gaze onto the invisible, where pageantry and lightning, earth, water, air, and fire are separated and ordered.

The woman is engaged differently on the path of love: what she finds in the man she loves is her image and her name as a woman. *Béatrice*. Through her, paths open up. Confident of her sexual identity, she expects from the man her place in the corporeal order and her function in the grammar of the idiom at hand. Mainly, however, she always hopes that giving her her name and informing her image is first of all, on the part of the man, a recognition of her identity as a woman and of her initial and ultimate familiarity with the truth of castration. Nothing of what she can expect from the man—and she expects everything—is receivable except in addition to the recognition that she is a woman and speaks from a place of sexual certainty. For her, *jouissance* is where she encounters the names and images of the phallus in the man. All that the industrious activity of the male displays, like so many offspring of repressed phallic authority, offers her the visible, concrete, recognizable mediation through which her meeting with the double positively clinging to her body, her unsettling and familiar *Nebenmensch*—the phallus—will take place. But for this really to happen, for her to find *jouissance* with a man, she must successfully set herself free from the solitary escape always beckoning to her: she must stop investing her body as a phallic object, stop settling into a sturdy narcissism (in the ordinary sense of secondary narcissism) that takes her body as the privileged object of her love. Jumping ahead of the tentative desire of a man, she steals his gaze from him and gives herself the illusion of catching her *Nebenmensch* all alone, through the grace of her body. "I love and take care of myself, I prepare and adorn myself in trompe l'oeil with the radiance of my guardian angel. I am childish, seductive, beaming a smile of contentment with my womanly image; a bird in hand . . ." And voilà! She fools herself even before stringing along the silly man as he throws himself at the lovely creature. He, however, is only too happy to be given, all gift-wrapped and ready to go, the inviolable casket, sealed with the image of the jewel it contains.

> You love me for what I have made myself into. Of course I will remain unsatisfied, for in the lovely person where I took refuge, you don't recognize my original identity as a woman, and I can receive nothing from you, not even, especially not, *jouissance*. But if you dare not adore me as I am, then you don't love me, for I feel you want to destroy what is dearest to me, the image I have painted of myself, which must conceal, forever hidden, the wonder I am keeping for myself.

And the poor fellow, torn apart and rendered speechless by so much logic, proceeds to wear his heart on his sleeve, until, in a sudden burst of spite and rage, he finds another, a "real woman," built on the same model, of course. Such is the so-called narcissistic woman that ideology, flying to the rescue of these structurally victorious dispositions, offers the masses for consumption. She is also the castrating woman, not so much because of her gleaming teeth exposed by the smile on the poster, but rather because she keeps hidden from him the royal road to . . . castration.

And yet, even if she remains captive to her own traps, a woman, as the saying goes, is still a woman for a man who knows how to take her. But when a man is convinced he loves a woman, he is hardly clear-sighted, not to say a bit of a fool. With perfectly lame logic, he will protest his love by parading all of his phallic attributes, the pale offspring of a carefully buried black sun. "I love you," he will repeat. In a major key, he says, "I'll give you all I have, look and taste how fine and good it is. I think, I work, I produce, I own, and it should be obvious that I want you since I have a hard-on. You can count on me." In a minor key, as sincere as he is naively cunning, he says, "without you, I am nothing, a lost child, with no courage or desire; I need you. After all, it's simple: since I love you so, you have no choice but to love me." It is true that she finds in the man the shimmering display of the phallus's names and images, which enables her to take stock of the *Nebenmensch* haunting her and open the door of *jouissance*. Big deal, though, this offering of a plumage that, like it or not, is the stuff of every man! Naïveté is the only excuse for the insult. Just like an unstoppable child, sure of being in flesh, blood, and words the proof of the existence of the phallus, this somewhat limited lover makes a gift of his banality as if it were a wonder. But he is ready to proclaim love impossible if the woman he tries to seduce in this way does not respond with wild transports to his generous offer. Yet only a woman of small spirit can be taken in by such poor logic. Other lures, true decoys, are the stuff of love. Beloved, I give you a stone we saw together on the path: it is not mine, and with it I give you the sun, the moon, stars and sky, all that shines in you and is reflected in it, gray, azure, green, and silver, a token of *jouissance*, a silent thing that will never stop telling you, "I love you."

Perhaps I should write more on what loving means, especially the singularity of the features and their specific arrangement that determines, for each of us, the choice of the loved object: eye color, slope of the back, grain of the skin, flourish of the neck. However, not only are these facts part of common experience, where analytical investigation only brings a more precise light on the origin and fixing of the choice's determining features, it also seems that these operations are not fundamentally different for men and women. In other words, the logic of the phantasmagoric organization itself, through which desire is launched, differs no more than does a so-called woman's car from a so-called man's car: it is ultimately necessary to take the driver into consideration, the subjective position driving it, in order to find the sexual break.

The frigidity of the narcissistic woman cannot be resolved by taking apart the sole phantasmagoric implications that rule over the choice of sexual object. What is truly necessary is an analysis of the repression of her primary narcissism, supporting her position of retrenchment in the love of her own image. Similarly, the man's sexual failings cannot be surmounted without a radical analysis of his masculine position, which is entirely built on the misrecognition of castration. Many a time, a woman taking the man at his parading words, telling him she loves him and expressing it with a keen desire for the fiery glory of his erect penis, is enough to make it pale and withdraw. I love you, says the woman, and the man hears, not without reason, that he is loved not only for his plumage but for her expectation that his desire implies loving her, that is to say her sexual position and proximity to the phallus, which is what she offers him by loving him. But it is more than the straw man of a sex-ridden ideology can cope with. Rather than *jouissance* and a possible meeting with the phallic model, with the recognition of castration that loving implies, a debacle ensues. In it is born, if not legitimized, the distinction between desire and love, in a continuing misrecognition of castration. Worried above all about preserving that misrecognition, which gives him the illusion of being a man, a "real" man . . . , but is only a real phantasy, he will produce a very common symptom: he will say, "You see, I respect the woman I love, and I fuck the ones I don't care about." Desire and love are indeed different, but to make the exclusion of one the condition of the other is exemplary of the greatest impotence: not being able to face the truth of castration.

The impasses and failures of love are in many ways our daily bread. A great vigilance is necessary to undo the multiple traps hidden within the apparent complementarity of the sexes and the complex organization of heterogeneous dialectics between conscious representations, unconscious representations, and their conflictual ties and between the unconscious representatives and the phallic referent. If only in the statement "you are the woman that I love," elaborated naturally at the level of conscious representations, there remains some ambiguity about the possible predicates of *the woman* pointed to by *you* and stated by *that*. If, however, one switches to the level of unconscious representatives (signifiers), the statement breaks up and unfolds as "to kill," "that I have," "tail," "starve."[2] In the same way, we frequently find the image of a knee (*genou*) in unconscious representations, bringing together the entire enigma of the couple: *je-nous* (I-we). Finally, if one takes into consideration what each unconscious representative carries in terms of its phallic imprint and intrinsic heterogeneity, "I," "you," "that," or "woman" take their consistency from a more radical split than that of their ambiguity of meaning. More than one beautiful soul can get lost in this labyrinthine complexity, and the most passionate lovers will find a mine of pretexts for their arguments.

The traps laid out by the complexity of the structure are not alone in closing off the impasses of love. There is also the weight of prevailing ideas, the models of men and women suggested and imposed by any society: no matter how genial and valorous these model women and men may be they can of necessity only be perverted substitutes for what each of us has to invent in order to live.

We have no choice. No ideology, even of beneficent Nature, no philosophy or religion—no matter how insistent their pressure—can exempt us from our destiny. Blindly, full-speed ahead or going backward, in spite of all our good will or against it, on the web of all the divisions, infinite variations of the same story are woven, a story always already begun and forever to be unfinished. Each of those we allow to be written will bear a name: its seal of truth will lie in its being double, from a man and from a woman.

§ 3 Thérèse,
or the Death Drive

"Paid," the first word of any epitaph, gets inscribed even before "here lies." We live in a situation of insolvency: our conscience urges us to pay off our debts, while our unconscious gives us evidence that we cannot free ourselves from them for lack of an identifiable creditor. The story never ends. The account is never closed. Nothing will enable us ever to settle up with the missing creditor. Say what you like about the death of God, having killed father and mother and done away with the tyrant we are still burdened with an account to settle. But with whom?

And yet, Thérèse feels released. She was still in the cradle when her mother died, and her father disappeared during the war. Unlike many of her sister orphans who don't succeed in killing their dead parents, Thérèse seems to have duly buried them and completed her mourning according to the books. Neither the organizations that took charge of her nor her guardian were ever the object of conflictual passions on which unfinished mourning might have focused. She is lucid, clear-sighted, and efficient in enterprises carried out without more than ordinary problems. What then makes her come to analysis? Precisely her apparent tranquillity and a very keen feeling of having no debt or arrears, of having drawn a line across her history—which she knows well and can recount without difficulty—a very clear-cut line with no balance outstanding. Even her love life is peaceful, made up of trustworthy, lasting half ties, although short of anything definitive. No arrears, but it is as if ballast, fetters, and foundations were missing. Nothing betrays this lack of foundations except an instability, more cyclical than reactional, in her moods. She delayed starting her analysis, procrastinated, and went out of her way to get me to tell her that in all "conscience" there was no point in embarking on this adventure.

Two sequences, maybe three, each repeated many times, gave us the opportunity to cross the line drawn in her settlement of all accounts. The first sequence is from a dream: a sumptuous carnage of policemen, soldiers, and SS troops more or less disguised under other uniforms. The dream is always of the same type, in that the events leading to the massacre are simple and quick. In contrast, its detailed representation is worthy of the best-known battles in the history of painting, with Thérèse randomly battering to death and hacking to pieces everything that moves and finally, with unmitigated satisfaction and the hope they are still alive, tearing the guts out of everyone within reach. She does not hide from me the thought that getting her hands on me in the same way would give her at least as much pleasure. She is sincere, without a shadow of guilt.

The second sequence repeats itself in her professional activity, where she is brought into contact with persons who, without saying anything in a complaining, threatening, or conspiratorial mode, have decided to kill themselves. She has never been deaf to their secret; quite the contrary, she heard them with surprising acuteness, but she has also never been able to put the people around them in touch with the imminence of their acting out, as if she could not bring to her lips something of what she was sure to have perceived. As a result, time and again, a weight haunted her to the point of torment: might she not be guilty of some failure?

The third sequence, more blurred if not more uncertain, finds her in the family circle of her brothers and cousins: Charlotte with the children, even-tempered, happy, and peaceful as ever.[1] It's a miracle for the children, who are never so well behaved, imaginative, and playful. For her, it is the high point and almost the reward of the week. Held back by her faithful half ties, however, she will probably never have children of her own; she may even, without perceptible secret drama, not really want any.

How could one not see that these idyllic children's games and parties are today, without the least distance of memory (where would it come from?), the hours of light and peace she finds week after week as what is not accounted for in her settled accounts? How can one not tell her that what she is unable to communicate about the imminent death of the persons she is listening to is the effect of her denial of any debt. It is the echo, in the other, of what she is convinced she has killed and buried of herself. What she lets come to light in these dramatic circumstances is a moment of suspense in which death was not certain, and when she could have said to the person about to kill himself: who exactly do you want to kill? She cannot utter this question, for she cannot even question how her story has been stamped "paid," supposedly settling her unconscious debt and closing up her anonymous creditor in vaultlike oblivion. And finally, how can one not see that she is endlessly busy settling accounts with the tyrant, quite nicely indeed, and not recognize an inexhaustible liability enacted in the elaborate massacres she repeatedly indulges in in her dreams? There she finally rediscovers the passion moving her, even in the paradoxical but peaceful arrangement of her life.

That score can never be settled except falsely: the killing called for can take place only by missing its victim, so that the demands of the debt and the successful killing are constantly repeated. They are the source of our life, as tenacious, determining, and present every minute as a visceral hatred. More powerful than "loving thy neighbor," this pressure to repeat forces us to live every instant of our story. Freud called it the *death drive*. What has to be put to death are the constructions and phantasies claiming to account unambiguously for our filiation, or, more precisely, focusing on a single point the source of the forces moving us. We truly are both "sons of God" (but it would be better yet, in keeping with the Old Testament, not to name Him) and His murderers. *What we must bring about so as to exist is our absolute separation from the phallus.* *At the same time, however, what we cannot erase in ourselves is the figure of that phallus*: circumcisions, baptisms, and initiations are only its intensified seal, be it taken as redemptive, propitiatory, or preventive. It sticks to us blindly but we must rid ourselves of it in order to recognize it. A passion for living moves us like a forever powerless yet victorious effort to free ourselves nonetheless from what is hooked to each of our words and glued to each of our cells: this devil of a phallus, from which we have to separate and "dissex" ourselves if we want to have any reason for living and hope for *jouissance*. This is the unthinkable object, the ongoing work, the always focused-on goal of the death drive.

Like the faces of God (or the devil), the images of the phallus are many, especially since none fits, and every story shows us new ones in which it is enshrined. Our task is to reduce these endlessly renewed figures to masks. But what can be more frightening than a burning or decaying face, even if Beauty's features are to emerge from those of the beast?

For Pierre-Marie, the figure of the-child-kept-alive-for-his-mother's-solace has power over his life and dictates what, without exception, he *must* do. From a certain point of view, this is a relief, at least for a time. As the touchstone of his unconscious, the primary narcissistic representation of Pierre-Marie-the-consoling-child rules like a king by divine right over the life of his subject. Enthroned by the mother's phantasy and invested with phallic dignity, it rules with all the "originally" repressed representations over the ferocious logic of a system that remains invisible, inaccessible, and untouchable: the unconscious. Its power is reinforced by the ignorance of its subject; all it has to do is to say "since you are immortal, you will live, love, and speak in your name later on, when your mother is dead and your children and grandchildren have also become faithful and submissive subjects," and Pierre-Marie will start obeying unquestioningly, *perinde ac cadaver*—unless a symptom, in an insidious but persistent return of the repressed, shows up to suggest that in such kingdoms, subjects can only be subverted ones. This perturbation will intimate that the unconscious hideaway giving the tyrant his power necessarily divides the subject between his status as exile and his identity as a proofless witness of castration. In Pierre-Marie's obsessional neurosis, the symptom supports the subject's subdued but ferocious revolt from within his hideaway. In his phantasy of perfect obedience to the primary narcissistic representation, violent and vengeful sequences erupt: parades of savage murders and blind destruction from age-old war epics going back to lost ages . . . , which leave the phantasized fortress and its regent untouched. Thus, Pierre-Marie imagines bloody orgies in public transportation or peaceful professional meetings where he attends under false pretenses. What he really wants by means of these massacres is to settle accounts with the little creep Pierre, his dead brother.

For Thérèse, the figure to unmask is the line drawn across her story in settlement of all accounts, a hard task if there ever was one since the line seems to indicate that she succeeded in the impossible feat of really killing the tyrant. She therefore appears to be living with the peaceful conscience of someone who has done her duty and eliminated the ghosts of the past. But this is no more than a solid alibi, artfully put together, in which the powers of the unconscious, gathered together in the extreme opacity of a single line, create a falsely transparent illusion and focus, like a cheap glass bauble that only sends back reflections, while letting nothing or very little show through. The false crime is almost perfect, and Thérèse is nearly taken in by the deceitful cutting edge of its line, to the point of pretending to forget that the tyrannical unconscious representations are intact and as voracious, alive, and savage as in their first blush: her devouring mother devoured by illness; her father giving life and exterminated; Thérèse victorious and abandoned, all hate and sweetness, ready to love. These elaborate dreams of carnage will lose some of their charm and effectiveness. In order to look at and properly honor these unconscious figures now that she has found them again, she will have to kill them individually, one by one, with no hope, for all that, of thereby paying off her debt.

∿

Pierre-Marie-the-consoling-child and Thérèse who makes mincemeat of people out of love: these two tyrannical representations must be eliminated. But how? The powerless weapons of dreams fire in vain on these phantoms: pierced through with bullets, torn apart by grenades, roasted by flamethrowers, they mockingly go their merry way, endlessly defying us. In fact, other weapons will be needed to kill them. First of all, we must realize that what is thus thematized as a revolt, a fight to the death, a vengeance to unleash, is but the phantasized elaboration of our forced relationship with the unconscious representatives that determine and make us up in the same way as our genetic heritage or biological givens.

But the unconscious is governed by a logic different from the logic of statements (the legal tender), which does not mean that it does not follow any logic. Freud formulated its principles in a striking summary:

> There is in this system no negation, no dubiety, no varying degree of certainty. . . . In the Ucs there are only contents more or less strongly cathected. . . . By the process of displacement one idea may surrender to another the whole volume of its cathexis; by that of condensation it may appropriate the whole cathexis of several other ideas. I have proposed to regard these two processes as distinguishing marks of the so-called *primary process* in the mind. . . . The processes of the system Ucs are timeless; i.e. they are not ordered temporally. . . . The processes of the Ucs are just as little related to reality. They are subject to the pleasure-principle; their fate depends only upon the degree of their strength and upon their conformity to regulation by pleasure and pain. Let us sum up: *exemption from mutual contradiction, primary process* (motility of cathexis), *timelessness,* and *substitution of psychic for external reality*—these are the characteristics which we may expect to find in processes belonging to the system Ucs.[2]

It is immediately apparent that unconscious representations as such cannot be admitted into the conscious-preconscious system. They are unacceptable (*unerträglich*) not because of their contents but their nature; they are simply not receivable, in the sense that there is no place for them, just as you cannot have a fish live in a birdhouse. It is nonetheless quite an old dream to be able to meet in our own space beings who do not exist there, and fiction takes it upon itself to describe in great detail extraterrestrials, zombies, and other living-dead who, to our delighted "horror" keep on visiting our planet or haunting our houses. The unconscious representatives proper are repressed by nature, as it were, which does not stop them from existing, in quite an organized way, in their own strange system—the "original" unconscious.

The offshoots of these primordial formations are very different. They will fall under secondary repression, in the common sense of the word, and constitute a sort of second-generation unconscious.

> The second phase of repression, *repression proper*, concerns mental derivatives of the repressed instinct-representation, or such trains of thought as, originating elsewhere, have come into associative connection with it. On account of this association, these ideas experience the same fate as that which underwent primal repression. Repression proper, therefore, is actually an after-expulsion. Moreover, it is a mistake to emphasize only the rejection which operates from the side of consciousness upon what is to be repressed. We have to consider just as much the attraction exercised by what was originally repressed upon everything with which it can establish a connection.[3]

Before getting back to the "offspring," objects of secondary repression, another word on the parents. The formulation we can give to unconscious representatives (those that constitute the unconscious of the originally repressed) always resembles in some way the blurred photographs of UFOs, thereby testifying to the basic and insurmountable inadaptability of our modes of conscious recording to grasp the elements of the unconscious system in all their radical strangeness.

In my analysis of Philippe's unicorn dream, related elsewhere, I had occasion to produce a transcription of this nature, a sort of incantation: "Poordjeli." In order to distinguish the picture from the model, we will call the model, according to Freud and as we have already done up to now, the *unconscious representative*, and the picture, in this case Poordjeli, the *unconscious representation of the rep-*

resentative, or in condensed form the *unconscious representation*. Only through the slow work of analytical decanting could the unconscious representation Poordjeli appear. In fact, the entire work of analysis had concentrated, as usual, on the model for Poordjeli. The offspring all have traits in common with the original, which are essentially recognizable in their literal figures, in which OR, LI, PO, and JE come up constantly and insistently: Paul, George, Lili, *peau, corne, corps, or, rose*, among others.[4] They are also recognizable in a sort of scansion, in the omitting of the phrase's central articulation: Poord'jeli, Philipp' Georges, *Philipp' j'ai soif*.[5] And finally, at the level of meaning in the contents of representations, other common modes organize and enlarge the offsprings' family: *pied-tête, roc-sable, eau-boire*.[6]

These elements constitute the representations repressed by deferred action and on which the work of analysis takes place. They take on body and words in neatly identifiable figures and formulas such as "Philippe chéri," "trésor de Lili," "joli corps de Lili."[7] The unicorn, which appears in a dream, lifts the veil of a deferred repression and so has the privilege, in this case, of being the most striking analogue of the representation Poordjeli, of the originally repressed unconscious representative. On the one hand, in its name as well as in its figure, it brings together, displaces, and condenses, *as would the primary process*, most of the elements of the offshoots' family. In its signifying form, on the other hand, it mimics, like a counterpoint, the unconscious representation Poordjeli. The analytical process can begin only by working on the offshoots of the unconscious representative and deciphering the formations resulting from the deferred repression. But only by referring the figures revealed in this way—here the unicorn—to Poordjeli, the representation of the unconscious representative that engendered it through the series of its offspring, only in that way can the difference be marked between psychoanalysis and one of its most perverse bastards: psychoanalytic psychophilosophy. In other words, *taking the primary process as such into account is what defines analysis*. In so doing, it takes charge of its own irreducibility to any compromise that could make it "presentable," indeed "representable" in the realm of reason, or accessible to the limited view of "good" common sense.

So we see how the work of psychoanalysis searches for an approach, a way to locate unconscious representatives without claiming that any translation (or transcription) can be absolutely faithful. But it is not enough to describe the approach. It is also necessary, no matter how difficult the enterprise, to attempt a formulation of the unconscious representative's specific traits, as Freud started to do. *What constitutes its essence,* so to speak, *is its energy charge,* as if it were made up only of virtual space, without representable or representative content properly speaking, but where a quantity of instinctual energy arises. What the unconscious representation Poordjeli represents is indeed, as it emerges in Philippe's analysis, a driving impulse represented as a falling motion. But it would be a bit too simple to confine ourselves to this bodily motion, which only summarily translates the "instinctual motion" (or motion of desire) at the heart of the unconscious representative.

Each unconscious representative is made up of a "quantum of instinctual energy," but it would be futile to imagine that it can be propped up by an atom of conscious representation or a substratum of meaning. It can be identified only by two figures, or two letters, like blood pressure, which can be established only in terms of a relationship. So, for example, for the unconscious representative figured in the representation Poordjeli, the two letters are linked by a kind of syncope or omission: *d'j* heard when the phrase is pronounced. But this relationship can be found as well if we shift the stress in the same syncope to the ends of the phrase: P-L (*poli*), or in a fragment like J-L (*joli*), or by extension in the *li(t)'cor(ps)* of the representation, which underwent deferred repression.[8] This relationship is stably fixed only because of the permanence of the differential system of which it is both cause and effect, as well as the constancy of the force for which it provides the virtual place. Everything else about it is variable: the figures that attempt to translate it, the "quantum of energy" on which it draws, the representations that come to be inscribed on it.

The "instinctual motion" manifested in this way by the unconscious representative is to be thought of, to the extent possible, from within the originality differentiating it from physical models of energy. *The instinctual force* is to be conceived of as *the correlative tension of the different incompatibilities making up the "psychic reality,"* as an incompatibility between the conscious representations and the unconscious representatives (in our example, between "unicorn" and the unconscious representative) or between the representation of the unconscious representative, "Poordjeli," and the phallic referent. This incompatibility stems from the intrinsic heterogeneity of the phallic referent itself.

The incompatibility between conscious representation and unconscious representative consists of a twofold and contradictory relationship. On the one hand, the unconscious representative necessarily produces offspring, a sort of conscious inscription (even though it must undergo a deferred repression). Better yet, the unconscious representative tends to inform itself in the register of conscious inscription, here in the form of a unicorn, as if it had to sustain the indefinite possibilities of its mobility with some term other than the phallus. On the other hand, however, the conscious representation tends to void, erase, eliminate the unconscious representative, to the extent that once formulated and inscribed it imposes the negation of its intrinsic mobility. The variability of the differential elements making up the unconscious representative thus tends to be voided by the conscious representation. The unicorn freezes the live force within the indefinite possibilities of displacement and condensation inherent in the mobility of the elements of the unconscious representative. It reduces the possibilities to a limited number of definite figures: the connections D-J, P-L, and J-L, are denied the most of their potential variability. The frozen character of the representation tends to supplant the constancy of the force in its mobility. The unconscious representative is thus confirmed in its position as a radically repressed element: rejected, contained, denied its live force.

The incompatibility between the representation of the unconscious representative and the phallic referent lies in the impossibility for the unconscious representative of taking into account the intrinsic heterogeneity of the phallus, which cannot be reduced to a combination, variable or not, of homogeneous figures, P, J, D, L. This is because of the heterogeneous nature of the unconscious system's referent, which is simultaneously encoded as an irrational number *and* as the irreducible remainder of its division. Put another way, like the complex number $a + ib$, it comprises both its positive sum *and* the unthinkable negative unit: $i - i$. One can neither say nor think "phallus" without instantaneously going through to the other side of the mirror where *the object* without reflection shatters and melts the logic of the signifier. In fact, *the psychoanalytic concept* that *introduces this heterogeneity* in connection with the order of unconscious representatives *is the Lacanian concept of the object (a)* elaborated upon the Freudian notion of drive. One can say, moreover, that all these incompatibilities are sustained by, and derived from, the heterogeneity of the phallus.

We were saying that the instinctual force is to be conceived of as the correlative tension of the different incompatibilities that constitute psychic reality. Let us now add that it, as befits its "sources," is double and contradictory, or, we might say, divided and conflictual: the life and death instincts, as Freud ultimately named the duality of the forces that animate us.

The work of the life instincts can be seen in the apparently predominant organization of conscious representations. The instinctual forces said to be on the side of life are in some way centrifugal in relation to unconscious sources. They tend to valorize the positive terms of the opposition and to produce systems of representation and bodies of inscription whose primordial function is always to contain, to keep repressed, and to deny the "negativity" of the other terms in the opposition, as well as heterogeneity itself. They were called sexual instincts in the first Freudian theory of the instincts, and they display, as in dreams and phantasies, the singular features and specific mechanisms supporting desire: a woman's face with its outline and eye color related in a certain way to prominent cheek bones, a woman who may be the object of another man's desire. The life instincts are the ones that spin the imaginary web on which the reality of desire is woven. They produce phantasies of desire through which the offspring of unconscious representatives arrange allegorical representations of the quest for the phallus on a semiclandestine stage: the unicorn hunt or the quest for the Grail. But if the life instincts, confident of their conquests and yielding to the "imperialist" tendency of their power, relegate the keenest forces, known as death instincts, to the side of evil in hopes of eliminating them, then the fantastic, daily staging of desire sinks into the absurd, to the mockery of a bad caricature: as if in a bad musical comedy, the quest for the phallus becomes a singles' pickup scene or a computerized selection of the ideal companion. Correspondingly, on the official stages of public life, the appointed producer of the life instincts orchestrates other, more or less "sublime" representations glorifying creation, thought, ideology, science, where everyone is grateful to find the proof of the great destiny reserved for him by the organization: to be a puppet guided by the strings of a perverse tyrant, a glorious and abject figure of power.

"It is very difficult," Freud noted, "to come to a more or less concrete notion of the death drive." This is because the so-called death instincts tend to privilege what is "nonfigurative" in the unconscious representative and the unthinkable negative term, comprising the phallic referent. When this prevalence makes itself felt, it can only be experienced as putting into question, indeed ruining or destroying, the life instincts. This negative work clearly goes against the flow of thoughts, representations, ideas, and systems carrying us toward an ever more elaborate repression of the accursed part of ourselves, the nonrepresentable inscription. On the other hand, however, nothing can be written, said, or represented, if the force of the death drive ceases, even for an instant, to maintain a clear and structuring reference to the phallus. Since the primary function of each of the conscious representations is to bury and forget the uncanny mask of the faceless phallus, the work is interminable and the struggle constant.

If by chance the libidinal investment of conscious representations by the life instincts happens to be withdrawn or is missing, there will be a surge of *anxiety*: we are overcome by an excessive force that, for lack of some recognizable object (a), attempts to clutch at our very insides, breath, and heart, and through them at the hidden, nonrepresentable "soul." Although it is difficult to have a conceptual grasp of the death drive, we can at least experience its strength through anxiety. Hurled into a subjective panic, our only recourse is in a mouth-to-mouth, hand-to-hand, and word-for-word resuscitation of the conscious, which is to say libidinal, representations. And yet, none of these conscious representations can come alive and take its place in the economy of the libidinal figures spinning the web of our desire if the forces of the death drive cease to keep clearly distinct the unconscious representatives that are the building blocks of the unconscious system. If for some reason they come up lacking, the "psychic apparatus" starts to go *mad*, as if it had *lost its raison d'être*: the conflictual opposition between two radically heterogeneous systems. It is a madness manifested in various ways by a psychic organization (or disorganization) that is always characterized by an absolute denial of the intrinsic heterogeneity of the "psychic apparatus." The denied conflict may be projected, in the paranoiac mode, with aggressiveness, querulousness, or sensitiveness, into an irreducible "external" conflict between the autocratic power of an omniscient, all-powerful "ego" and the unfathomable stupidity and cretinism of others. The schizophrenic mode may instead place its cut—radical, sufficient, ravaging, or provoking—between a ghost self and a nonexistent world. The work of the so-called death instincts consists in constantly ensuring, against the formidable unifying tendency of the life instincts, the strange and singular presence of unconscious representatives and the absolute heterogeneity of the phallic referent.

Let us sum things up. For Pierre-Marie, the primary narcissistic representative as figure of the child-not-dead-for-his-mother's-consolation reigns tyrannically in his phantasmic life. For Thérèse, the deceptive figure of castration is the line drawn across her story in settlement of all accounts, compelling her to live a life of semi-

desire. Figures to unmask and figures to kill: the weapons of dreams and reason are powerless against them. We were saying other arms are needed: first of all, the realization that what is, in these cases, translated into revolt, a struggle to the death or an act of vengeance to assuage, is only the phantasmic elaboration of our compulsory relation with the unconscious representatives that constitute us in the same way as our genetic inheritance or biological features. *"To kill" these figures consists in giving back to the unconscious representative its true status and in taking into account the unmeetable debt tying us to the phallic referent.*

Practically speaking, this means recognizing the primordial, constant, and absolutely necessary force of the death drive. It is the death drive that in and through the figure of the tyrant to be killed, and the primary narcissistic representative to be destroyed, defines the place of the unconscious representatives as both one's native land of exile and lost paradise to be regained. It is the death drive that ensures, in a word, the presence/absence of the Other, without which there can be no speaking and desiring "I."

§ 4 Justin,
or the Subject

Justin can't bear what little play is left him by the feeling of being frozen into an image of himself by the gaze of another.[1] As a child on family trips, what made him sick was not the ride but the fact of having an assigned place in the family car. Letters pursuing him through changes of address enrage him as if he were being cornered by his written name. If a woman loves him, shows it or tells him so, he is ready to flee. One game, called tease or solitaire, fascinates him.[2] In it, numbers or letters are aligned by moving small square pieces, a shifting made possible by the presence of an empty square. Only when rock climbing does he feel distant enough from himself to open a gap in which breath and movement, if not words and his desire, might be born. This rigid, playless collusion that needs to be broken up is the statue, as dense as a bronze embrace, of his parents in each other's arms. Justin carries on his shoulders, like Atlas, all the weight of his embracing parents, a primal phantasy if there ever was one, bringing together the fallacious alibi of a long since dispersed family and its initial raison d'être. He lugs around with him, clutching his shoulders, the scene of his origin, hidden from view but present in all its weight: he rebels, kicks, and struggles, but can't throw off the obscene riders clinging to him. He needs a word to break the hold of the monstrous beast, but has none. "I have nothing to say," he cries with rage; I happen to answer him, "'I' has nothing to say." Without breath, voice, or space, he is trapped in the primal scene he bears without seeing. Its monstrous setup freezes the story in an extreme of denseness, and redundancy seems to block every possible move.

At the place of the solitaire's empty square, a leaden piece blocks the game: Justin feels turned to stone, as an aphoristic and immobile figure in his own story from which he cannot escape. The work of his analysis will consist in dismantling the phantasmic structure that contains all his violence and brings together his image and story in the extraordinary density of this burdensome, compressed figure. To burst the monstrous beast is indeed his wish, his unconscious desire, which surfaces in an emotional dream: preparations are being made for the solemn burial of the grandmother's corpse, but it changes into an enormous boar, a "solitaire," which explodes, giving off a cataclysmic stench.[3] Through this first breach made in the hold of the horrible, three-bodied monster blocking Justin with an extreme and painful back stiffness there appears the exploit of his adolescent father killing outright a furious old boar as it charged him. This decisive, head-on hit makes it possible to grasp the lost thread of another web, a secret romance, different at last from the family epic and the fabulous success already inscribed in the history of the mighty. Another story emerges, wild and full of risks, death, passionate violence, war exploits, madness, and love. In it shines a woman, the first wife of Justin's father, a person with no family name to speak of "but" passionately desired. In the web of words and representations in this parallel romance, the father is often in a position of power that, in the official story, seemed monopolized by the grandmother's lineage.

But mainly, with the new story, it becomes evident and hard to bear that his mother has never been more for his father than a substitute for this other, nameless woman. This new side of the true family romance will be unveiled through the analysis of an insistent memory: when still a child, Justin received a long, detailed, and unusual letter from his father, from a faraway country where he was exploiting new land by planting vineyards with imported vines. For a long time the analysis of this striking memory stumbled over the very writing of the typed letter, obstinately indicating that something in this message was written, marked, and printed for all to see. But what?: the vineyard cultivation to which the father was dedicating himself with fruitful passion. I learned, at the same time that it dawned on him, that Lavigne was the maiden name of Justin's mother: the couple's story was indeed written in the long message for all to see. Suddenly, the obscene beast on Justin's back seemed to have been struck and thrown off. Justin remembered violently throwing his father back to the nameless woman and turning the corner into another impasse, toward his mother, as if he could finally disengage himself from the hold of the primal scene and at last follow a banal oedipal itinerary.

This time around, another man's intervention was needed again for Justin to leave the kingdom of his mother. Peter's name came back to him, translated into a bottom-of-the-sea nightmare, like a disturbing call: "Pierre, Pierre, Père" . . . with Peter, he knew he could live, speak, and desire.[4]

A word, a few words, were needed for the play of his desire to begin, and it was moving to hear how accurate he was whenever he got lost trying to spell out what he was talking about each time he mentioned the game of solitaire or his being paralyzed by having so little play: *j-e* or *j-e-u*;[5] J (Justin) had nothing indeed, really nothing to say, even though he could speak quite well about the official story in which he was caught up; except for saying again and again how he had been compelled since childhood to resort to distressing symptoms, like overeating whenever he had a meal with his father, and then right away bursting and vomiting up the food that had taken the place of conversation, or, even today, painfully locking himself into his stiff back to speak wordlessly of his paralysis. Yet words are there, albeit, so to speak, mute. But at the same time that the other faltering, fragmentary, hesitant story begins to take shape, the unconscious begins to say "I," and the words begin to speak. Two stories, two texts, are linked as in a palimpsest, one of which maintains the image of Justin glued in the family album while the other comes to life by representing "I" in its movement.

Unlike those children of all ages who never stop saying *moi-je*
with the persistent illusion that with this expression they can resolve
the antinomy between the two ways of speaking, Justin can neither
lean on a "me" nor sustain an "I."[6] On the one hand, he can only
reject the clothes and hairstyle designed for him and leave the place
prescribed for him in the car, at school or work. He can only refuse
even more to recognize himself in the features that make him up,
be it the mouth he inherited from his mother, his father's courage,
or his nurse's tongue: in short, he can only mistrust all that might
set him up as a "me." On the other hand, anxiety takes hold of him
whenever even a hint of *jouissance* invades him, when a word opens
onto a double meaning, when the isolation of the *solitaire*, caught
up in the game, shines inside a diamond or bursts in the assault of
the furious beast. At least he does not doubt that to enable him to
say "I" is where analysis is leading him. *Wo es war, soll ich werden.*
He, Justin, knows without having read Freud, that "I" is not a "me"
and that the advent of the subject is neither the unveiling of a
statue nor the enthronement of a new prince.

The work of psychoanalysis, as we know, consists entirely in letting the unconscious speak, in somehow having the other story be
heard. But it is a singular story composed of erratic fragments: a
back, a solitaire, a smell, the space of a breath, a cry; it is arranged
like a constellation, impervious to time and events, in the shape of
a strange body that could never say "me," but articulates "I" in the
interval of each element.

To draw that body, write that other story, and have the scansion of the "I" be heard, notes (named with letters) would be
more adequate than words. At the end of the *Art of the Fugue*
manuscript, Carl Philipp Emanuel added the following remark:
"While writing this fugue, where the name of B.A.C.H. (si-la-do-
sol) is taken as countersubject, the composer died." So this coun-

tersubject appears as the final metamorphosis of the unchanging basic theme.

This basic theme determines the unity of the work up to its incompletion. The same notes, the same letters, make up the web and give birth to the fabulous display of fugues and canons. The calm and mysteriously stable basic theme outlines intervals of the fifth, third, and fourth, in a succession of confident and natural connections, as a rainbow splendidly displays the array of fundamental colors. They first combine in a reverse order, in opposite movements, in the simplicity of the fundamental, basic (diatonic) intervals. Then, very quickly, the infinite nuances of the intermediate relationships, of mixed (chromatic) colors, come into play as so many necessary and miraculous possible effects of the original theme. An anonymous commentator writes:

> The basic theme appears in the different fugues in various guises. Counter voices spring from it; it welcomes elements of voices from the counterpoint; it transforms itself through this vast process, like the human personality . . . it lives . . . Each fugue brings a different solution—in the conception of the whole form, as well as in the use of technical procedures—from the simple fugues (the first four) to the three fugues in opposite movement (in the sixth, the theme appears in diminuendo up to half of its rhythmic value, and in the seventh fugue, a double crescendo and a double diminuendo appear simultaneously) to the fugues with several themes, where new themes come to join the main one. In the double fugue, called "en miroir," the second fugue is the reverse image of the first: the basses become the sopranos, the tenor becomes the alto, the ascending melodic line becomes a descending movement with the same size of intervals. In the triple fugues, each theme is first developed independently (in all the voices), most often in reverse, and only after that do the themes combine. The last fugue was probably meant to be a four-theme fugue, since the existing three themes can easily combine with the basic theme of the *Art of the Fugue*, a synthesis that would have been the culmination of the fugue. It remained unfinished.[7]

In the same way as a basic theme, the—properly speaking—unconscious primal phantasy (Philippe's "Poordjeli" or Justin's back-solitaire-smell-breath-cry) is at work in the whole of psychic life. The subject lives in it. Each note of a basic theme (re-la-fa-re-do, etc.) is a model lending itself to infinite melodic, rhythmic, and harmonic variations. Similarly, each letter in *Poordjeli* (P-D-J-L for the consonants) is a sort of primal theme in Philippe's unconscious. We have already formulated a few identifiable variations. In isolation, each letter, each note, causes a series of harmonics to vibrate; inscribed in a sequence, each note assembles, contradicts, or calls on other notes' harmonics.

An open ear cannot but hear—if not know—that each note of the "well-tempered" scale, made up of equal half tones, is defined by taking no account of all the frequencies between the half tones, from the quarter tone to the imperceptible vibrato. Yet these virtual notes, not written in the tempered scale system, vibrate in its full-sounding harmonics and can even immediately be heard in such scores as J. S. Bach's admirable Suite for Violin Solo when they are correctly played. Brassens or Reggiani not only compose beautiful songs, they sing them as only they can, slightly off-key, each time the same and imperceptibly different, in short, with deeply moving accuracy. So it seems that each note of the tempered scale represents not only all the other notes of the system and the relation governing them but also, and at the same time, the intermediary, unmarked frequencies, excluded from the system. Accurately measured by a stringed instrument, the opening fifth of the *The Art of the Fugue*, re-la, leaves no doubt as to the mode in which it will be inscribed, even before the playing of fa, as if an imperceptible vibrato were already cut off from the "tempered" la to announce the fa of the minor third.

Thus, it is more apparent in the system of Western music than in a spoken-language system that the set of elements making it up is defined by what it does not take into account and that it only comes to life by somehow taking back what it excluded. Only one system fulfills the conditions necessary to sustain this contradiction: the unconscious. The name of the function maintaining the contradiction is the *subject*; fascinating in its division, it focuses all the effects of oneness. Through the subject, what the system of representatives (number, note, letter, or signifier) had excluded from its web as it was being made is taken into account; at the same time, the meaning-making "I" is called into the line of splitting that characterizes the subject.

For the exegete who cannot resist imitating the work of the unconscious, variants, erasures, mistakes, and, to his torture, lost outlines are all intrinsically part of the finished text. And yet the printed, delivered text only got written at the cost of all these losses. Actually, the unconscious does not only take alterations into account, as one likes to imagine. Even more radically, it takes stock of what gets lost in the process of inscription, what drops away as a result of a cutting edge of sorts, in the stroke making the changes. In the unconscious theme Poordjeli, a hint of this reject can be perceived, for example, between D and J, whose syncope or apostrophe makes something of the raw edge of D emerge. In it, *je*, in suspended breath, seems to be heard even before J comes into speech. *Nothing* can represent the fall line, and yet each letter (each unconscious representative) sustains it as its own limit or margin. The unconscious system is made up of an indefinite number of representatives (signifiers) *and* of what is rejected by the play of their reciprocal determining. In other words, the fall line, which separates, as would the cutting edge of a guillotine, what will remain inscribed from what will never be, is far from being itself rejected. It will maintain the essential and absolutely specific function of the unconscious system, that of *subject*: as much a point of nonsense as of sense.

What characterizes the unconscious is that each of its elements (representative or unconscious signifier) not only functions in a mechanistic system, as the representative of other elements; above all, each element also represents the cut that made it free of any excrescence or smudge. "I" lets itself be heard—without being able to speak—at the same time that the unconscious elements appear in the first theme, recovered by the analysis of the phantasmic formations. For they never stop expressing, in the light they project onto one another, the darkness that makes them shine and the ungraspable line of sunrise that separates them from it. Heartrending as a cry, uncertain as the crack of dawn, the subject withstands nothing less than a splitting, the splitting he ceaselessly ensures, to no avail, between the signifier and its remainder. The subject of the unconscious system, long before being a grammatical function and far more determining than a philosophical concept or a psychological instance, opens up the space of speech. Not that it speaks. At most, one can say that it desires: from the raw edges it is busy cutting, antinomic forces spring up from this "movement called desire," itself split between the fascination of the lost remainder and the attraction of the permanent, unconscious mnemic traces (signifiers).

The *remainder*, separated as it is from the primal unconscious inscription, is pregnant with ambiguity: it speaks both of its vocation as refuse to be discarded and of its destiny to remain. So one can only conceive of it as faceless, wandering with neither hearth nor home, outside of that indestructible first dwelling, which is not the phantasy of the mother's womb but the erratic monoliths of unconscious mnemic traces. Arranged according to a secret topography like a field of menhirs, these traces are beyond the reach of both memory and oblivion. The offspring of the subject of the unconscious—the ones on their way to becoming society's good subjects, the "me" of neurosis or the shadows of psychosis— make no mistake: they take good care of the remainders. One zealously collects cocktail coasters; another loves "fine books" and gathers the frayed edges of the folio pages he delights in cutting. How many good homes overflow with scraps of all sorts? More telling still are these unsettling shadowy subjects who put away their nail trimmings in little boxes and who even manage to collect their feces when they aren't trying, as we know, to hold on to them inside themselves. A reasonable person will say, "Come on! That's no good. It's not clean!" It must nevertheless be granted that, however laughable, this is an eloquent way of mimicking the kind of unconscious subjective activity that constantly lends support to the split and disdains objective reason to uphold the nameless dignity of the remainder, the real of the margin. It is in there that the subject's very traditional puppet remains, nameless and placeless: *the object* in its primal darkness.

The unconscious thus reveals to analysis the least graspable of its component elements, the object as its share of shadow, as dense and unnamed as the very substance of our body: a substance that, within its recognizable elements (members, organs, or nucleoproteins) makes up the body's irreducible burden of real. It is there, beyond any wholeness, that what constitutes the body is first found, like an obscure pain or unnameable pleasure, as if, from the start, the body's initial burdens were expelled into the margin: the call of hunger, the aching need to sleep, the tightening of a spasm, the squint of an eye before it can make something out. The beyond of the margin is peopled by shadows, nameless pieces of body constantly struggling and quieting down. It is a chaos of pains and smiles that nothing can ever put in the "right" order. Be it hell or a garden paradise, it is from this nonplace, haunted by pieces of the "primal" body, that come all the anxiety and *jouissance* in the world. The bursting of Justin's solitaire and Renaud's imaginary visceral wound had already led us, with their aura of honor or disgust, to the limits of the object's kingdom. It is from there that the instinctual objects, all-powerful viceroys, come back: breast, shit, gaze, voice. They divide the land, our bodies, and our "souls" among themselves. Naked in spite of their regal robes, they rule with sovereign power.

There is no immediate access to this forever unknown continent, although it is called "primal." It remains forever to be discovered in the entanglement of body and words. And no one but the subject knows its borders, for the subject is the one who never stops deciding and cutting, separating and tidying up the order of words (first of all the order of unconscious representatives, signifiers in the Lacanian sense) so that the now indivisible (not guilty) scraps that make up the all-powerful force of the real can be relegated to the order of loss, of the unnamed. We know or reject the subject only as our double: an unsettling shadow or body of light, the mute guarantor of our words, the prerequisite condition of the play (as Justin would say) of the forces of our desire.

~

Contrary to treaties establishing peace, *the subject vouches for a constant struggle between the colonizing power of words and the revolt of what is rejected.* The cause upheld is simple: to demolish the overwhelming, totalitarian representation capturing the individual in the eyes of others as an apparent, indivisible whole. No, "I" is not that. Justin cannot bear to be assigned to one place, reduced to the indivisible unity of a character in the family epic; he is paralyzed by it, suffocating, dying.[8] Actually, it's an old story that is constantly repeated for each of us, in the cradle, at school, in the family, at work. And how nice it usually is to give in to the orderly play of the grand comedy that assigns costumes, roles, gestures, and lines to all of us—soldiers of all ranks, choirboys or notables, grassroots militant or M.D. psychoanalyst belonging to the Ecole freudienne de Paris! Fortunately, like children facing a policeman, robber, or puppet show judge, we keep bursting out laughing. It's an old story, and with it, everything begins again and again: a child to kill, our delivery to go through. Always already caught up in a dreamlike third person (he will be a great man, she will marry a prince . . .) and in the seduction and bidding of a second person (will you answer my wishes? are you coming?), the story starts only in the first person: no, "I" is not that. The subject is born and re-born solely from a constant disentanglement of body and words, from a perpetually repeatable crossing of the grid of signifiers, from the ghostly, hallucinated reunion with the lost but immediately present object, right there, so very close to us. That object has no image nor any possible representation in the margin of figures and words, in what is forever closing and opening the doors of our body. It is the pulsing of our desire.

Justin has a passion for a certain kind of geography, which he fulfills with a taste for mountain rides and hikes. As fragmentary signs of that interest, his dreams reveal rugged cliff roads along the sea, cut off by falling rocks, that, however, he still manages to drive through, as well as high mountain peaks he finally reaches only to find, much to his surprise, a pasture rolling softly into the ocean. Over and again the main road of his dreams takes him to the nameless woman. Above all, a valley seems to separate an exclusively maternal massif from the realm of his possible life as a man, which he reached through Peter. We can recognize another, related form of passion, as recognizably his father's from what he reports: a passion for land. When he is not clearing some in faraway places to plant vineyards,[9] he is busy reviving and exploiting vast domains where, incidentally, he lives: to each his exploration or exploitation of the land, his clearing of a field or deciphering of a topography where each of them is constantly looking for the other. To recognize this feminine or maternal land, as Justin does with extreme reticence, is still to say very little about the secret of the fields of inscription it conceals. It is, however, the first recognition of an essential fact: that the necessary crossing of the signifiers' grid, which enables the subject of the unconscious to be endlessly reborn, does not happen by chance at just any point in the universal nomenclature.

In confronting the mountain, at the right distance from the rock, which time and again ensures the effectiveness of his hold, Justin finally finds the play, the leeway that makes him into "I" in a surer way than in any other circumstances. For him, the steepest and hardest spot on the rock (of castration?) is where he is sure of having access to the gap in the system pinning him down. But how can one not hear this as an acknowledgment of his filiation? For his father, it seems that the confrontation with the cryptograms of virgin or fallow land was the means of realizing the crossing: for him, it is there that a sort of renaissance occurs, a coming into his own, a recognition of his secret name. It happens there in a surer way than in his social successes or amorous adventures. The ancient figure of the plowman, unexpected in a man of his standing, is also his unconscious phantasy. Without even knowing it, he imposed its mark upon his son more firmly than good manners, for sure. Now, in contrast to the other viselike ways in which Justin feels victimized and trapped, the chain of unconscious representatives in his father's phantasy, even as it imposes its power, opens up a gap: the cut of the subject crossing that gap. Justin will turn his father's "clearing the land" into the privileged instrument for killing his primary narcissistic representative, the child-Atlas caught in the impasse of his parent's marriage. In this place of power or weakness in his father's phantasy, in its secret name, Justin's "bodily deciphering of the rock" will be born, and he will practice it by decoding the succession of holds that will open the way to the necessary rape of the rock.

These related terms, *clearing the land* and *deciphering the rock*, are, of course, merely the representations of the unconscious representatives properly speaking, which can be written in the sparest way as D-CH-F-r or D-F-r-CH.[10] These unconscious "primal" themes are equally capable of producing such representations as "cart's fire" or "crapping in the frock." In each of their renderings, these themes present a live opening onto the lost part whose representatives are cut off as they are being inscribed. In contrast with the offspring of the originally repressed, whose themes and elaborated variations (a taste for hunting, an interest in typography) fill in the gaps in the subject with various ornaments, the "primal" theme is stripped by analysis of the secondary elaboration's overload, letting the gap in the subject appear at each scansion.

Through the family romance, weaving various themes from collective myths and individual phantasies, Justin feels caught in a tight web without light or air, which paralyzes and stifles him. To analyze it is to light up the web, to bring it back to its original, strict, but widely spaced stitches, able to both hold on tightly and open up to every crossing. In the last analysis, however, it is mainly up to the prisoner whether the net becomes his trap or support: caught in the totalizing illusion of the oneness of the self, he will fall captive, like a battalion taking itself literally for a unit and maneuvering as one, in tight rows inside a fortress, thinking it is besieged by open doors. If, on the other hand, he recognizes, as analysis demands, that unity is but a fiction and a "body" always fragmented, the grid of signifiers will not impose itself as in a siege. It will instead become the texture beyond which the object (the partial, separated, lost object "a") remains hidden, and through which the subject, as a double agent, can sneak over the wall.

~

Thus occurs "the advent of the subject," the very essence of an analysis. Through necessarily slow work on the secondary phantasmic formations, the original unconscious themes are uncovered. In them there appears, stripped of the chatty histrionics of the large family of offspring, the play (or "I") of the subject struggling with the irrepressible, shadowy power of our double:[11] the real, nameless body of our instinctual demons. Over this pandemonium of instinctual objects, the god phallus reigns, unique and testimony to order. His power comes from a grain of light,[12] transparent and rough, glowing with signifiers like so many moons and hiding the objects in its dark shadow. In its extreme transparency and evanescence, like the soaring arrow of the lark drawing the azure of its song, he commands the field of love.

§ 5 Sygne,
or Transference Love

Even the slightest clue to what I am most interested in cannot escape Sygne's notice: in my office, her sovereign gaze uncovers the gold nugget and the glittering of the geode's hidden crystals; in my writings, she unerringly unties the phantasmic web; and from the mess on my table, she tries to decipher my worries and projects. I have never had a more attentive or penetrating analyst. What is at work in her vocation of "researcher"[1] is obvious in this "thirty-year-old woman"[2] whose familiarity with numbers led her very early to Science's discreet honors. With the signifying clues about me that she collects like precious honey through her secret computer, she tries to shore up and sustain the wild flow of her representations and satisfy her thirst for love. Through what she identifies, rightly or wrongly, as the representatives of my phantasies, she tries, as did Justin through the grid of his father's signifiers, to open up a gap in the space of a sigh, a rest, a haven. Her head, where words are constantly marching by like numbers, is full of the teeming work of a life in gestation. To better express her demand, she imagines resting her forehead on my marble mantel piece or wooden table, just as she would like to let it sink into my hands, just long enough to be silent while I take charge of the exhausting round of words.

Although she manages only with the greatest effort to *support herself*,[3] indeed even to *stand up*, Sygne is forever *backing up* her family, holding the little ones with her voice and gestures in a way no one seems to know anymore, attentive to her brothers for whom she can find the single word that can clear up an impasse, present at death's door as only someone who is trying to be born can be. It seems that between us there is something like words, or better, passwordlike names, those of newborn children or dead relatives. As close as a relative, she knows my family's birthdays and wonders about my descent, since she can't wonder about her own. Are not Freud, Boole, and Einstein our common ancestors? She would have liked to know me in my "oedipal" age. Looking at the picture she has constructed of my four-year-old self, I cannot *resist*. Letting the last remnants of my doctoral respectability turn to dust, I rediscover, without concealing my smile, the seriousness of that age when one knows what it's like both to desire passionately and to suffer. Through that smile, whether it lights up the eyes or the voice, another ear opens to which the pain of being nothing and of being born of nothing[4] can at last be told without pathos, in the voice of truth. Between two strokes, between two words, what remains silent (the *infans* rather than adorable cherub) gives *room* at last to what could not be said. It is there that transference takes shape. Sygne puts it in figurative terms: your smile in your face, my pain on your face, your pain on my face, my smile on my face.

I don't believe in the neutralizing illusion of the impassive mask and in this instance find no need to defend myself against what could be construed as seduction. Analytical listening implies bringing into play the spot of silence that is the place of transference. What is given there is the space for an act of real intelligence in terms of the logic of exclusion, a passage beyond the web of representatives, a way of passing through the mirror. The analyst's presence, kindness, neutrality, and silence are merely inadequate or approximate ways of marking this point of no resistance to which his own analysis must at least have brought him, with no turning back. Whether we call this, paradoxically, conscious awareness or describe it as the advent of the subject or the recognition of castration, what we can absolutely demand of an analyst is a knowledge of *what speaking means*, what decisive shadows words can hide, and how they can show the subject crossing their web. To have experienced it is to discover, in repeated phantasies, their forever new grains of origin. It is to set free what is locked up in our knowledge; in dealing with our analysands, to recognize without holding back what cuts to the quick—in short, nothing less than to take account of the unaccountable, to perpetrate the death of the word-image and to undermine the all-powerful unconscious representative. These are necessary operations through which the (re)birth of the subject can be realized. Words are prey to the universal work of repression in which every family unit, group, or social "order" takes part, and they never stop reverting to muteness. Only by giving the most vigilant attention to questioning the unconscious representative, and above all by calling into question the tyrannical primary narcissistic representative, can speaking be kept alive.

Here another side of the killing-the-child phantasy is revealed: by naming the child *infans*, the discourse of repression pounces on the fact that he does not use words, so it can make of him, unfairly, the one who does not speak. It is true that it would be convenient for princes, parents, and teachers of all sorts if each "subject" were only to repeat faithfully what he is told and if the child did not disturb the order of repression by speaking the truth. "Be quiet, you don't know what you're saying" is what the so-called analyst repeats in his own way when he orders magisterially, "Speak, *I* know what you are saying!" And yet, well before a child can put words together, he speaks and lays bare what speaking means, in an orgy of jubilation and rage, smiles and cries. The little interloper must be made to behave, to look, precisely like the picture of good behavior:[5] a first killing perpetrated well-meaningly and in good conscience and whose result (the very image of a nonspeaking *infans* or repeating parrot) will constantly have to be killed in order to retrieve what it represents through its fascinating image, in renewed power and engendering force.

My psychoanalytic raison d'être can be formulated at this point as an interest in the "origin" of speaking (castration, primal scene, death instinct). It is an interest that can admit of no distance, so truly taken am I by it, with no question of being able to discard it or choose another object of inquiry. Engaged in the analytical experience, I rediscover, as alive as ever, an insatiable, childlike "curiosity" about origins. I have other means of satisfying it, but I am not sure I know any better than a child how to sustain the urgency of the question: from recovered memories to relived traumas, from realizations to scientific progress, from oedipal configurations to Lacanian algorithms, I never stop answering it, even at the risk of bringing it to a close. And yet, I remain an analyst only to the extent that I listen to the analysand from this gap through which speaking and desiring are constantly reborn. Only in that space can the subject's syncopated voice be heard and the singularity of the analysand's "primal scene" be told: his "origin," that is to say the particular mode of his hold in the order of words, the singular ordering of his connection with the silences of the first objects. To be an analyst is to remain in the gap and keep it open, in fact to keep alive, like a desire, the interest that made us "enter analysis": How does the unconscious speak? How does it desire? for me, for him, for her, for each of us.

The history of psychoanalysis and the Freudian epic must be seen above all as stemming from this dauntless "curiosity," an "adventurous road that had scarcely ever been trodden before,"[6] leading inexorably to the edges of the forbidden lands where desire is born. "It will be a fitting punishment for me," says Freud, depressed, "that none of the unexplored regions of the mind in which I have been the first mortal to set foot will ever bear my name or submit to my laws. When breath threatened to fail me in the struggle I prayed the angel to desist, and that is what he has done since then."[7] The adventure cannot take place by proxy but only with one's guts and soul exposed. When about to finish *The Interpretation of Dreams*, Freud says it and then dreams about it: "None of my works has been so completely my own; it is my own dungheap, my own seedling and a *nova species mihi*."[8] "The task which was imposed on me in the dream of carrying out a dissection *of my own body* [the reference is to its lower part, pelvis and legs] was thus my *self-analysis* which was linked up with my giving an account of my dreams"—the secret of dream interpretation and desire."[9]

But nothing can ensure the analyst against the risk of filling in his listening gap—neither the analytical institutions whose fate is rather, in the process of defending Freud's discovery, to ensure the extinction of any curiosity, nor theoretical formulations as written guarantee of the spoken word. This necessary inscription (grammaticalization, mathematization) cannot ensure access to the other "inscriptions" in the form of unconscious representatives but could, on the contrary, be a substitute for them. Nor can the analyst's analysis, even ongoing, be any insurance against the sealing effect of an insidious phantasy of mastery or "end," which can, for example, take the familiar form of deciding to sit in the analyst's chair.

I am quite willing to recognize that my way of inscribing and describing the analytical process carries with it, as does my practice, the stamp of my own phantasmic perspective and that traces can be found in it of a few determining signifiers in my destiny. But what matters to me is that between my words, through the organization of my discourse, in my interventions or silences, space for the navel of dreams remains free and gates open onto the night. In that space, Justin says that his father wants to clear the land and that in passing through this fundamental phantasy his own passion for deciphering rock takes root.[10] There, he can also discover the silence of his mother's desire. In that space, Sygne says that roaming signs and the impossibility of rest undermine her, burdened as she is by the weight of having to guarantee words and their defects all alone, without phantasmic parents. In the silence of my listening, she quiets down. In what she can grasp of my desire's representatives, she takes root.

The analyst's wager in the curing game consists in putting on the line his questions about the origin of speaking. It involves progression, invention, and mobility, as opposed to the apparent immobility of the analyst's chair. In counterpoint to the welcoming effect of silent listening, uninterrupted spoken words break away, bypass their object, and respond to the incessant question of their origin. A sharp ear makes possible this commitment to hurling oneself headlong into words and the intervals between them, into inter-diction proper. This is a necessary and expected condition outside of which analysis runs the risk of merely being a conceptual elaboration as foreign to instinctual reality as picture-words are foreign to truly speaking. It is a necessary and expected condition outside of which transference would not be this irreplaceable place of truth and would be no more than the occasion for a powerfully suggestive hold.

What every analysand commits to analysis is his hope, however ambiguous, of even partially getting out of the discourse of repression in other ways than with symptoms. If we ignore our wager's demand for truth, which opens up the space of transference, we cannot legitimately sustain our refusal to respond to the analysand's demand and truly keep listening to desire.

Already we must go beyond what in primary narcissism and the death instinct is tied to the primal phantasy of "a child is being killed." As the kingpin of analysis, transference raises the question of the secret phantasy that makes the analyst become a demon hunter attempting, in the *hic et nunc* of the session, to awaken the unconscious representatives and their prodigious fruitfulness. Light can be shed on this strange destiny only by questioning the "birth of psychoanalysis," in other words, the profound passion that drives the discoverer of enigmas and the explorer of origins in the extraordinary Freudian adventure. That passion is manifest at once in the intensity of transference. It took all Freud's determination in the face of Emmy von R.'s demand for love to bring about the birth of analysis. The fact that analysis was born of Freud's impassivity in front of women's desires in no way allows us to reduce his perplexity to blindness; it merely forces us to take up what is unaccounted for and upon which all discoveries originate. The silence of the enigma "What does a woman want?" remains for psychoanalysis as it did for Freud the price paid for the oedipal discovery.

And yet, as we never stop going back to the origin with certain of our female analysands, unless we take refuge in deafness we male analysts can only experience that "we have no right to dispute that the state of being in love which makes its appearance in the course of analytic treatment has the character of a 'genuine' love."[11] Furthermore, nothing allows us to pretend that it has nothing to do with us, that to take a woman in analysis has nothing to do with any kind of seduction or, especially, that the interdiction we set up along with the analytic relationship shields us in any way from the risk of loving (rather, the opposite). But it has to be recognized that apart from referring to it under the vague heading of "countertransference," analysts keep very quiet about their "temptations" as well as their guilty love affairs. Let us at least grant to Breuer, Freud's companion at the start of the adventure, the merit of having perceived the problem clearly: in the face of "temptation," he left for Italy with his wife . . . but did not discover the Oedipus complex.

Must we conclude, as does Eugenie—a woman questioning herself about her position as an analyst—that to become an analyst today suggests some profound powerlessness?[12] She declares abruptly that it is always so as not to have to screw. She is not merely giving vent to a so-called vexation, as one could easily "interpret" it. The familiarity with castration that the analyst's "job" demands is too often used as an alibi for a false mastery. What we can easily discern through the inconsistency of pretentious shadows that many supposed analysts have taken for a religion is the pure and simple avoidance of castration or, surreptitiously, the acting out of its denial. According to Eugenie, psychoanalysis has a paradoxical tendency to be the place where fears of sexual difference and of woman conspire most firmly to maintain their hold. And yet, if one had to conceive of a place where a woman's words could be heard, I don't think one could make it more transparent and faithful than the place of transference. *What a woman wants is first of all to be recognized in her sexual identity.* Love, be it courtly or flirtatious, romantic or "free," is not always enough; to be taken by a man, even very lovingly, does not necessarily guarantee the loosening of the repressive discourse's grip (socialist as well as bourgeois!) marking a woman at her birth and in the course of her history.[13] We have seen that the discourse of repression, endowed with a universal calling and masculine par excellence, is built on failing to account for "half the sky," so that no woman could possibly recognize herself in it. However loving a man may be, since he is implicitly responsible for this forfeiting of *jouissance*, it takes great courage for him to halt the effects of his mischievous complicity in the universal enterprise of repression.

Historically, this is where psychoanalysis steps in, but these days it seems to be having some trouble living up to its calling. Indeed, above and beyond her supposed vexation, Eugenie is denouncing the following major paradox: whereas at its origin the destiny of analysis was to ruin the constantly renewed effects of repression, it is now slowly but surely getting caught up in the dazzling blindness that presided over its birth. Under the guise of an *Aufhebung*, it is also laboriously reconstructing a system to take over the other "half of the sky."

But for now let us limit ourselves, along with Freud, to not denying that the state of love appearing in the course of analysis has the character of "true" love. This fact is more than enough in itself to keep us busy since it confronts the analyst not so much with the impossibility of the undertaking as with how extraordinary it is. Let us go directly to the essential facts, at least in the case of some female analysands: not denying the nature of true love is only a careful way of stating that one recognizes love, and this, of course, is the least one can expect of an analyst. This is not the time to yield to philosophical or aesthetic temptations and think of love as a winged Cupid or a concept. What we need to recognize—so long as we also refuse to deny it in similar cases to those who presided over the birth of analysis—is *the love of a woman*. What do we mean by this, if not that our answer will depend, eminently so, on this inescapable recognition? But how?

Regardless of the secret of the analyst's phantasies, I will leave in the shadows of conventional discretion cases in which the practitioner, although an analyst, is still no less a man and, without more ado, seals his recognition with a "carnal act." The analytical adventure usually leads us further. Recognizing transference love as real means first of all that we somehow wished for it. Seducers in our own way, we have invoked the infernal powers and conjured up *hic et nunc* the demons of love.[14] Invited to speak her peace, sooner or later, a woman will inevitably express what speaking means for her, namely, that *there is jouissance.* As I stated in Chapter 2, "for the woman, not only do words, above and beyond their signifying functions, keep their value as unconscious representatives, as signifiers of *jouissance,* which will constitute her woman's word. In the immediacy of her connection to castration, she also finds support for a process of properly sexual identification that first specifies her as woman before any secondary identification of a trait or figure as belonging *to* womanhood." What she expects from analysis is what a man of today, for whom identification with ideology's representations takes the place of a sexual position, seems most often unable to give her by the mere homage of his power: the recognition of the essential truth of her words as a woman. What a woman wants is first of all a man's recognition of her woman's words, since its durability is not originally guaranteed by any repression. Essentially, her words retain their position of unconscious representative (signifier) and only incidentally enter the system of meanings. They are the stars and glorious bodies of the phallic system and can speak of nothing more than the shadowy place of any body's objects. She expects man's discourse to pin to a screen of repression the signifier of her glory in the flesh and have it be his hope of seeing a piece of the sky.

Just as she does with numbers in her work, Sygne in analysis uses words to speak of love. The breathless round of signifiers she sets in motion speaks of nothing but her pain, or rather, her *jouissance* in suffering.[15] She is not fooled by it. Her wish to rest her head in my hand and lean her body against mine is not—at least she says as much without further denial—to appease her desire; rather, it is to find bodily consistency and anchor for the words haunting her, a shaded, cool spot for the fires of truth consuming her. When catching hold of the signifiers she imagines (most often rightly) to be those of my desiring phantasies, she is not merely asking me not to disown them but also to be faithful to them. It is as if the constellation of my unconscious representatives, set like jewels on the screen of all my repressions, could give her support by recognizing her as Sygne.

I have no doubt that some doctors in psychoanalysis would tell me that I should have received her in an office more bare, that I should not have released my writings as I have done. They might also advise me to further analyze my phantasies so as more carefully to avoid such countertransferential implications. They will no doubt think that my paying more attention to the analyst's legendary discretion would have spared Sygne her entanglement in a transferential rapport that I will have a very hard time "terminating." Besides loathing this term,[16] I refuse to believe an experience of truth can ever be erased: transference is such an experience and so is transference love. It is not just my supposed indulgence that allows Sygne to grasp the signifiers of my desire. My accepting her into analysis is an invitation to speak, and she is going without detour to the end of what she has to say: her *jouissance* in suffering. In so doing, she loves the person who invited her to speak and lets her speak. Everybody knows that the most definite symptom of love is the acuity enabling the lover to go to the heart of the loved one's signifiers, however strong the resistance. Now let us suppose that, following Breuer's example, I indulged a reaction of withdrawal in front of a woman's love and labored to convince her of its illusory or pathological nature. My interventions, even if pertinent and sober, could only be taken for what they would in fact be: a blunt refusal, a way of telling her that, even in analysis, a woman's words of *jouissance* have no place.

Nothing seems more essential to me, in the practice of analysis, than to refuse to take part in this sort of betrayal. Of course, I don't fail to ask Sygne about her former loves, especially her childhood ones, and to remark on the inconspicuousness of phantasies of her parents, to the point of summing up her oedipal situation to myself as a sort of deficiency of phantasmic parents. I could never take advantage of my analytical function, however, to tell her anything that could be construed as denying recognition to her love, her woman's word. Now I would be in bad faith if I pretended that Sygne (to speak here only of her) leaves me cold. In this love story, my whole life resonates harmonically: not only my loves, women's words (or silences) inscribed in my body, children, but also my interest in analysis, my questioning the origin of speaking, my work on the discourse of repression, my quest for half the sky. Does this mean then that I love her? No, that is to say, not "really," but it could have been, outside analysis.

If Freud had not been busy with Martha, his fiancée, he would have discovered the anesthetizing properties of cocaine, and one can suppose that his so profoundly masculine passion to be a discoverer of enigmas would have been appeased for some time. He might not, however have discovered the unconscious. What is extraordinary about the analytical adventure is revealed in this meeting between the discoverer and his true object: love, which is to say a woman's word. A strange and familiar woman's voice! We will see in the postscript to this book, "Vienna, or the Place of Births," what, over and above the phantasy of the killing of a child, is revealed in the secret body of birthplaces. We may also guess at what it is in the most secret of the analyst's phantasies that incites him, like Freud, to attempt the impossible unveiling and reinvent psychoanalysis. Analysts, and Freud first among them, are as suspicious (or clear-sighted) as Zeus and fear their sons will kill them. Wishing to give birth himself, power-hungry Zeus swallowed his first wife Metis, pregnant with his child, when time came for delivery; and so it was that from Zeus himself, from his head split in two with an ax, intelligent and powerful Athena was born, fully armed.

So Freud discovered the secret of dream interpretation, gave the unconscious its status, and formulated a first law of desire in oedipal terms. But he held onto another, still questioning She-Sphinx: "what does a woman want?" There can be no more "innocent" discoveries, but here we are, analysts confronted with a demand more acute than in any other endeavor, to reinvent our practice every time, word by word. Analysis can exist only when a meeting of two nascent voices occurs, indeed, as in love, but with naked words and benumbed bodies.

∾

By the way, what is the sex of analysts? Do they have one? The question is worth submitting to the next council. Today, the prevailing opinion is that indeed they do, but that it doesn't matter as long as they have ears. The answer might as well be no! I can't resign myself to this. To maintain that an analyst's sex has no immediate bearing on his or her practice would be tantamount to turning the analytic function into a sort of priesthood placing the analyst beyond the plurality of the spoken word, especially the duality of masculine and feminine voices. I know that the phantasy of a universal discourse is indestructible. This is because it upholds what is most derisory in man's claim to "virility." But I think I have shown sufficiently how the temptation of a universal discourse is part and parcel of the work of repression and that it is never anything but an attempt at subsuming all the modes of repression. Let us recall just how much this enterprise turns out to be masculine, since for lack of an immediate connection with castration (which for a woman essentially determines her identification as sexual) a man will find sexual identification by breaking with the process of repression that he inevitably leans on for support. The superfluous and pitiful "*I* am a man!" is always marked by some spectacular violence against the order to which he is a secret accomplice. Just as there is no metalanguage, there is no Esperanto of sex, in other words, no pseudoanalytic discourse capable of going beyond difference. Quite the contrary, what we call analytic discourse promotes another logic (from the unconscious). It is defined by taking castration (connection to the phallus) into account, and castration is what determines sexual identity in speaking beings. Analytic discourse leaves to each and everyone, starting with the analyst, the task of knowing from whence he speaks.

At least four figures are essential to account for the diversity of transferential situations and analytic adventures. A woman's words offered to the ears of a discoverer of enigmas cannot be kept as the only implied model, for this lone reference could lend credence to the image of analysis as a man's business. For example, a young woman came to see me after long years of analysis and serious studies at the Ecole. There was every reason to expect her to practice analytic listening with a great deal of talent. But even though she had been trained as an insider, she felt she was a woman nonetheless and was downright terrified by the "analytic abjection" that tends to hold sway among the newly ordained.[17] She said she felt like the talmudic scholar overwhelmed with knowledge, who went among the people crying, "Quick, quick! Ask me questions, for I know the answers."

Perhaps, along with other women, she will be able to show us two new figures of transference with its traps and privileges: the male discoverer of enigmas displaying his talents on a woman's couch, and women together, so wondrously strange and familiar a sight for a man.

And then there is the man who "wants out"—meaning of repression—and comes to me as to a brother. Here I am at last confirmed in my status as doctor of the unconscious, interpreter of dreams, destroyer of repression, and discoverer of forgotten memories. Vigilance is required here, so as not to fall into a parody of analysis. It's easier to imagine a game of love between a woman on the couch and a man in the armchair than between a "psychiatrist in training" and a "training analyst." But what is at stake in analytic theory or its institution, in a phantasmic woman or a question of power, implicates men no less *in a love story*. Whether the lures of these stakes are recognized or denied (or both), transference is under way as soon as we meet the request of an analysand with a decision to engage in analytic work. By elaborating on the analysand's connection to castration, we have to put our own on the line and shed light, beyond homosexual phantasies, on the lack of the phallus. This is a matter of *jouissance* if ever there was one. But that is when the cunning little god bristling with learned arrows will not fail to corner us in subtle impasses where passions put on their shows. The burden will be on us, Hermes or Aphrodite, to sort out what speaking means.

To each figure its own traps but to each its own promise of truth: as alive as at the time when analysis was first invented, the hope for *a voice to be born* is always there. Its engendering is more hazardous than giving birth to a child and can only be conceived of in an encounter with another nascent voice, which analytic textbooks label "interpretation in transference." But no marked or plotted path can ever tell, before or after, of the clearing brought about by the meeting of a voice open to innocence with the unveiling of its origin's syncope.

The analyst's attention, floating like a spirit above the waters, is first of all an openness to the transparency of words, their shadowy roots as well as their fruits of light. The follow-up to that story will tell us what price analysts are paying today for the sacrilegious obstinacy driving them to take the place of the Holy Ghost, and if, away from the armchair, they will still know how to experience love with naked bodies and veiled words. Not that among themselves they will invent "some new way to make love."[18] But one can hope that, sustaining the excess of their unreasonable passion to the end, they will at last know the time to love. Perhaps that passion, recognizing on the Tree of Knowledge the fruit that makes her a woman, will be able to nourish a man with her light, like a new Eve taking shape from words rather than from his ribs. Perhaps that man, gazing away from the clock that measures his listening, will realize at last that he can only love and give the dawn back to each day if, like Kronos, he devours his children.

Postscript: Vienna, or the Place of Births

by Nata Minor

Meetings with the uncanny are meetings back to back.

While tempted to write on Freud, Arthur Schnitzler, and their Viennese destiny, I can't quite make the detour. Is this chance, mirage, or wandering? the echo of two nascent voices? second sight, the business of the double? Renaud happens on this path.

Do we know if Oedipus wandered around the She-Sphinx before answering, or was it enough simply to see her profile and hear the sound of the air being displaced by her words? He may just have told her what he had always known and, to do that, could look straight at her, as there was nothing strange about all that. The uncanny story was familiar: a tragic story that could be spoken.

The connection between Freud and Schnitzler can be seen as the acting out of a fascination and an avoidance. Like a lost reflection on the slanted edge of a mirror, it marks the element of the unconscious that cannot be grasped, much less spoken, and never ascertained. Perhaps that is why repetitions, parapraxes, and slips constantly punctuate the text that I once devoted to Freud and Schnitzler, to the latter's short story "Nothing but a Dream." It took several years and my present work for me to realize that I was pointing to Vienna as Freud's native city.

The fact that this slip went unnoticed by alert listeners and readers would place it in the realm of the not uncanny, if it did not lead us to take note of how our thinking stumbles and falters when it has to do with Freud and the Family Romance.

Vienna, Schnitzler's birthplace, not Freud's, takes up little space in the latter's writing. He speaks of it only the more to hold it in contempt. It would seem that, with only one exception, Vienna does not appear on the list of the capitals he dreamt of so much when they were remote and avoidable. Yet what efforts he made to conquer it, to make his mark and stay there!

The fact that he lived there while denying it any charm, as if he had been asked to close his eyes, is astonishing and makes us suspect the existence of a deeply buried inner Vienna that points back before Freiberg, to Jacob Freud and his father.

How brightly Vienna must have shone when seen from a Moravian ghetto! How privileged a place it must have had in the dreams and longings of the little Jacob. Wasn't it to him that Freud wanted to offer this beautiful, unexplored ancestress? To give her untouched, however, it was necessary to keep the right distance and deny its seduction.

But if Vienna indeed seems to be the oedipal debt paid by the first analyst as a child to his father's unconscious, it also appears to us as a metaphor for a secret, different, difficult story, a mirror's secret where body and image look for and defy one another.

In one of Freud's dreams, Vienna is where Fliess is going in July. The dreamer wonders and free associates: "Why July? It's Julius Caesar's month . . . Julius, my younger brother, who died when a few months old; July, Julius' month; Vienna, Caesar's city. If he is Caesar, I am Brutus."

The month of Julius and the Caesars, the city of Julius and the Caesars, of fathers and sons, of fathers mourning for their sons and also of parricidal sons. To succeed where fathers have failed, to be like Caesar: every woman's man, everyman's woman . . . one man's woman? To have revealed to one, on July 24, the secret of dreams and to give birth to the immortal work that will perpetuate his name; but to do that, one must draw from what is deepest in oneself, *in one's own body*, dreaming and dreamt, as in the dream of the "anatomical preparation" where Freud meets with "the eternal feminine" in his associations while traveling inside himself. It is a voyage to the center of the body, of the earth, where the stops are not the expected ones and the rails extend backward. But let us go back to Freiberg. Freud left it when three or four years old. Many discoveries had been made already, many answers already given to unformulated questions. And the episode of the woman he refers to in his letters to Fliess as "my first inducer of neurosis" or "my professor of sexuality," an old and ugly servant, a thief and dealer finally "put away," this episode is surely not unconnected to his later question, which no answer will ever satisfy: "What does a woman want?"

That question is precisely the one that Schnitzler's heroes are untiringly asking. Dreamers without eyelids, they cross the city, rummaging through houses, imploring, demanding. They play games of chance, go to strange celebrations, remove masks and tear away disguises, question the morgue's silent bodies or the smile of their sleeping wife. And despite the answer *"Ich weiss nicht,"* "I don't know," inscribed for their author in the name of a loved woman, Olga Weissnix, they insist and persist.

"What does a woman want?"
But what do these men want?

This question is more relevant to what for Freud and Schnitzler was both a meeting and a nonevent than a parallel destiny, identical origins, shared interests, or troubling coincidences.[1] Vienna, as we said, is surely the capital of this nonevent.

The imperial Vienna as recounted by Schnitzler—seductive, depraved, mean, and fond of pastries—is close to the "Golem's" Prague, where the double circulates and projects itself freely. In that particular Vienna, half-open doors expose women's bodies; sons look obstinately for a message, the key to a secret, mostly the same secret that made Freud hesitate when, taking up the study of femininity, he declared it to be a "dark continent." To pursue his journey as explorer of the "infinite impasses," Freud needed firm ground on which to rest. Any splitting of that ground provokes vertigo, a blurred memory, the uncanny.

When the first American astronaut came back from the moon, everyone could tell how pale he was. To the question "what did you see?" he answered simply, "I saw God and she is black" and collapsed.

In "Rosa or Men's Happiness," an entire regiment is swallowed up and disappears in beautiful Rosa's welcoming body. Maurice Pons does not tell us if, on the way, he meets with the horse that, in a shorter but not better story, a rider looks for in vain.

In 1895, Freud was present when, in the course of a small operation on the sinuses of his patient Emma, a bandage was extracted, which doctor Fliess, a bit of a dreamer, had forgotten there. Freud felt faint at the sight.

Fainting, uneasiness, novels, and anecdotes, so many dams to contain what is not understandable in a woman. But is it really about her, and is she the only one concerned?

If we kept to the interpretation of Schnitzler's story, "Baron Leisenbogh's Destiny," that Freud gives us in "The Taboo of Virginity,"[2] we could believe it, and it would in fact seem to us that the hero's fatal destiny is woven by the woman he just possessed. But if we go back to that story or others by Schnitzler, we see that neither the woman's cruel words nor her murderous intent nor even the secret supposedly hidden in her body actually ends the heroes' lives. They all die because of an other's words. A prestigious, gigantic, invisible Other whose project the woman harbors. Object of desire, agent and guardian, the woman is also the place of a meeting and a projection. Through her, men seek each other and invest her with wishes that she will realize: sexual and homosexual wishes, death wishes. Each sees and recognizes himself.

Someone said to Schnitzler, "It's not surprising that you became a great writer. Your father was already holding a mirror up to his contemporaries." The mirror, Freud points out, was the laryngoscope invented by Arthur's father.

After this witticism and the story of a mirror that Dr. Fliess also held up to his contemporaries, many years went by before the name of Schnitzler appeared again in Freud's writings. There is a note in "The Taboo of Virginity," and suddenly a paragraph about Schnitzler's "Die Weissagung."[3]

Neither a mediator nor a guardian, a woman passes furtively through this story like a suggested vision, a fragrance, or a color. Strange story, uncanny indeed, where man's destiny is drawn by an illusionist and unveiled in reading a blank page in the wake of a blown-off wig. It evokes in the reader something like the memory of a trace and in Freud the feeling of being mystified:

> When the writer pretends to move in the world of common reality . . . and brings about events which never *or very rarely happen in fact*,[4] he takes advantage, as it were, of our supposedly surmounted superstition; he deceives us into thinking that he is giving us the sober truth, and then after all oversteps the bounds of possibility. We react to his inventions as we would have reacted to real experiences; by the time we have seen through his trick it is already too late and the author has achieved his object; but it must be added that his success is not unalloyed. We retain a feeling of dissatisfaction, a kind of grudge against the attempted deceit; I have noticed this particularly after reading Schnitzler's "Die Weissagung."[5]

So there is dissatisfaction, feelings of rancor, no "incitement premium," no "fore-pleasure" or "the true enjoyment" that "proceeds from the release of tensions in our minds" brought about by "the writer's putting us into a position in which we can enjoy our own day-dreams without reproach or shame."[6]

Nothing like that follows from the reading of "Die Weissagung," only the feeling of having been mystified and gone astray into some false identification. Let us say we are fascinated, like the confused clients of an illusionist, or the heroes of Schnitzler's story "Fortune," where there is no woman but where the essence of the feminine seems to have migrated toward another place, another citadel, a place of mystery and shadow, an inner citadel. The man will look to himself, to his own likeness, to find the face to which he grants so much knowledge, his Mephisto, his pawnbroker, and will always end up evoking "the Eternal Feminine."

In "Fortune," Waldein, an artisan, is accosted one night by two strangers, counts or barons, in a Viennese bar. They tell him to follow them and offer to take him to the Jockey Club, where only the aristocracy is admitted. Drunk and bewildered, he lets them. They dress him up and drag him to the club, where he is introduced as a noble stranger from far away. The man plays and wins, plays and wins again. He breaks the bank, gets up and leaves.

When he wakes up, it's already getting light. Little by little, moments from the night come back to him, first vaguely, then more and more clearly. He goes to the mirror to make sure it isn't a drunkard's dream. He looks at his reflection and recognizes the beautiful rumpled coat and white tie; also, his hair has been cut.

Where did he put the money? No, not so fast. He will look for it in a little while. When at last he looks for it, the money can't be found, and he can only painfully remember walking in the night, as well as a few clues: some disconnected cobblestones, a bush, a garden, and a murmur of water nearby. He rushes into the streets but they all look alike and the bridges are alike and the gray stones of the quays encircle the running and bubbling river . . . but where was the murmur of the water, by the way? In the second part of the story we find Waldein after he has given up his search. Old and sick, he is still vegetating in the same hovel. Neither his wife, now dead, nor his son Frantz, who became a painter, ever knew of his adventure, the strange meeting, the sealed fortune, or his forgetting of the place where the elusive fortune lies, what in the adventure cannot be named. Frantz carries in himself a secret he ignores, one that murmurs and besieges him but is not his (or is it?). On his canvases, he repeats one scene and only one, of players, a green rug, a disreputable bar.

One day an art lover, a rich and distinguished count or baron, comes to him and introduces him to the club to sketch a painting he wants done. In a large room, four gilded mirrors echo the shimmering reflections of the lights. There are tall figures with gardenias in their buttonholes. Prestigious and laid back, Count Spann is there. Around the carpet, faces are impassive, but Frantz can guess there is passion under these masks. . . . If only he could feel the same thing, play with them . . . create. With eyes half closed, Frantz Waldein dreams, "he feels he is entering into the secret, coming closer to the truth."

But what truth? What is this strange, singular secret from far away that he thinks he recognizes? Is it someone else's secret? Is it his? What prescience is there in the play of mirrors?

It is morning. The old Waldein is dying. Frantz is watching over him, afraid of falling asleep. A blue ray plays along the windowsill, lights up the vials near the bed, and makes the lips of the sick man even more pallid. "Unconsciously" and for the first time, Frantz sees himself finishing his painting. Memories come back to the dying Waldein; the water murmurs, the echo answers, the noise of a hammer is close to his ear, and suddenly the Lions' Bridge looms up.

Now the son knows everything. He runs along the river banks, unearths the fortune, hides it under his coat. He hurries back, but to a great silence: "No answer will be given him any more."

On the very day of the funeral, Frantz Waldein goes to the club. One word from the count enables him to play. I must, says Frantz, experience once what these people feel, enjoy with them the fire they are consumed by, take away the spark and then . . . *create, put out into the world the immortal work* that will pin down in a painting the place of seduction, the moment of *jouissance*: his father among these prestigious and affluent men who took him like a thing, who played with him a game he allowed and enjoyed, or else dreamed of enjoying, in ignorance of an insane project.

A sketch, a painting, an immortal work all hide another story, mask another place to which man can only get closer at the cost of his life or reason. At least that is how the phantasy speaks—the phantasy, or Schnitzler, or both.

Each of us carries with him throughout his life a part of the turmoil of his progenitors' unconscious secrets, and *the turmoil occasioned by the feminine part of the father* is not the least persistent. It is muffled by our personal noise and is difficult to perceive because of our projections, so it is hardly a murmur when it reaches us. Schnitzler, aware of this, gave us a story staging *the destiny of someone who unknowingly tries to grasp what the feminine essence is.* Projections and identifications mix, and the reader, in the wake of the hero, is pulled toward a place of malaise and extreme vulnerability. It is a voyage to the center of the body, of the earth, where desire is questioned and no answer is satisfactory. It is a shapeless, colorless, diffuse phantasy, and approaching it only makes us fall deeper into the cocoon of family romances. It is a programmed universe, with interchangeable slots, in which taboo and castration limit wandering and protect the illusion beyond which an elsewhere begins that no word can describe.

Once the game is over and the loss of the fortune consummated (whose prohibition is transmitted from generation to generation), Frantz goes back to the river bank where he digs around wildly, harvesting the fruits of another heritage: a bit of earth, a few stones, and murmuring water. Frantz has become old and insane in a few hours and gives Count Spann, who does not leave his side, the spectacle of a son transformed into his father who lulls his pain and cries over his child.

There is something like a wound between them, going back and forth, and no one knows where it belongs.

But where does the letter written by Freud in May 1922 to his disreputable colleague and neighbor Arthur Schnitzler belong? It was, after forty years of distrust, a birthday letter answering another and was followed by only one meeting (an evening with the family, an hour-long walk) after which they parted, back to back.

> To Arthur Schnitzler
> Vienna IX, Berggasse 19,
> May 14, 1922

Dear Dr. Schnitzler

Now you too have reached your sixtieth birthday, while I, six years older, am approaching the limit of life and may soon expect to see the end of the fifth act of this rather incomprehensible and not always amusing comedy.

Had I retained a remnant of belief in the "omnipotence of thoughts," I would not hesitate today to send you the warmest and heartiest good wishes for the years that await you. I shall leave this foolish gesture to the vast number of your contemporaries who will remember you on May 15.

But I will make a confession which for my sake I must ask you to keep to yourself and share with neither friends nor strangers. I have tormented myself with the question why in all these years I have never attempted to make your acquaintance and to have a talk with you (ignoring the possibility, or course, that you might not have welcomed my overture).

The answer contains the confession which strikes me as too intimate. I think I have avoided you from a kind of reluctance to meet my double. Not that I am easily inclined to identify myself with another, or that I mean to overlook the difference in talent that separates me from you, but whenever I get deeply absorbed in your beautiful creations I invariably seem to find beneath their poetic surface the very presuppositions, interests, and conclusions which I know to be my own. Your determinism as well as your skepticism—what people call pessimism—your preoccupation with the truths of the unconscious and of the instinctual drives in man, your dissection of the cultural conventions of our society, the dwelling of your thoughts on the polarity of love and death; all this moves me with an uncanny feeling of familiarity. (In a small book entitled *Beyond the Pleasure Principle*, published in 1920, I tried to reveal Eros and the death instinct as the motivating powers whose interplay dominates all the riddles of life.) So I have formed the impression that you know through intuition—or rather from detailed self-observation—everything that I have discovered by laborious work on other people. Indeed, I believe that fundamentally your nature is that of an explorer of psychological depths, as honestly impartial and undaunted as anyone has ever been, and that if you had not been so constituted your artistic abilities, your gift for language, and your creative power would have had free rein and made you into a writer of greater appeal to the taste of the masses. I am inclined to give preference to the explorer. But forgive me for drifting into psychoanalysis: I just can't help it. And I know that psychoanalysis is not the means of gaining popularity.

> With warmest greetings
> Your
>
> Freud[7]

Odd letter to send a stranger! Everything seems to be said, yet the intimate character of the confidence reinforces its equivocal nature and leads us to wonder what in Freud is shaken at the mention of Schnitzler or the idea of meeting him. Is it the latter's sensitivity to "the truths of the unconscious" or his focusing on "the polarity of love and death" that give us a feeling of "uncanny familiarity"? And of what is this familiarity made up? To what common phantasies, or phantasies considered common, can one refer it? To what evidences does it lead the reader?

Freud writes in "The 'Uncanny'" that "it often happens that neurotic male patients declare that they feel there is something uncanny about the female genital organs. This *unheimlich* place, however, is the entrance to the former *heim* (home) of all human beings, to the place where everyone dwelt once upon a time in the beginning. . . . The unheimlich is what was once heimisch, homelike, familiar; the prefix 'un' is the token of repression."[8]

The uncanny then may be "a hidden, familiar thing that has undergone repression and then emerged from it . . . such as repressed infantile complexes, the castration complex, womb-phantasies."[9]

The place allotted to the presence of the feminine body in Schnitzler's stories is quite striking. It can be evoked by a word, a poetic sentence, or a silence, traced like a filigree through every page, and courts projection, just as the work itself does. The author becomes a marginal, seductive character one cannot associate with, a "double" that the ego must "project . . . outward as something foreign to itself."[10]

In the work already mentioned, I wrote that this insistence on the maternal, feminine body, as well as a profound intuition and a certain mise-en-scène of the unconscious dealings regarding the inside of that body, are the basis for the uncanny feeling that beset Freud when reading the stories of his double. The uncanniness and fascination are triggered by phantasies that are all the more familiar since Freud was not spared their violence and which, in more ways than one, made him retreat when, in his writings or that of others, he chanced upon them. It is as if their unveiling put an order into peril and threw a doubt on the illusion they were covering up.

I will add to this hypothesis another one that is but a complement to the first.

It is a suspicious hypothesis in that it is arrived at through the confusion caused in us by the tumult of our begetters' unconscious secrets, a tumult that our own rumbling stifles or deforms. It is difficult to take hold of this hypothesis and formulate it in that it can only tell a parallel story, its only support being the fragile chain of our associations. One of the links in that chain is the letter to Schnitzler.

It is also an equivocal hypothesis in that it touches on the feminine part of the father, the feminine part of Freud, which acts as a stumbling block and a trace of some ancient revolt, some secret certainty in the face of a neither acceptable nor accepted death. A feminine part does not mean homosexuality, immortality does not mean megalomania, and the real does not mean reality. All three entities are carriers of an order that puts its stamp on the oedipal configuration. It is a singular order, itself marked by the stamp of desire while escaping its law. Located beyond the oedipal structure, it is the last bastion where the unconscious speaks, bleeds, and misunderstands.

That border is where the shadow of the pretenses evoked by Schnitzler is wandering about. Freud came close to that shadow. It follows him along in his work. It lulls him in his sleep. In the dissection dream, in the associations and interpretations that he gives, a lot is said about it, and it is not for nothing that the letter was written after the publication of *Beyond the Pleasure Principle*. It is a letter to the double, a double letter like the one that begins *Wien*, the repressed town, and in its essence it contains its own repetition, its own reflections and mirrors. It also contains the tenuous echo of a deep inscription, a birth mark, an ungraspable and constituent stamp of a generative matrix lying somewhere in the body, which has forgotten where, but around which memory never stops probing.[11] Double V.,[12] *Fau, Frau,* Faust: here is that other double where the wish of eternal youth meets with the "Eternal Feminine."

After all, the best of what you know
may not be told to boys.[13]

But each of us is his own pupil, and this letter, which strikes us
like a return to sender, gives us an entrance into the heart of an
ambiguous exchange where death wishes are right under the surface and where the secret remains whole in spite of its avowal.

"Old Brücke must have set me some task; STRANGELY ENOUGH,
it related to a dissection of the lower part of my own body, my
pelvis and legs."[14]

And Freud obeys. Louise N. assists him. In the recalling of what
occasioned the dream, Louis N. asked for and refused a book he
was offering her.

"Lend me something to read," she asked.

He brought her *She*, by Ridder Haggard, "a strange book, but
full of hidden meaning," and started to explain to her: "The eternal feminine, the immortality of our emotions."

"I know it already," she said, "have you nothing of your own?"

"No, my own immortal works have not yet been written."

"Well, when are we to expect these so-called ultimate explana-
tions of yours which you've promised even *we* shall find readable?"

"At that point," Freud goes on, "I saw that someone else was ad-
monishing me through her mouth and I was silent. I reflected on
the amount of self-discipline it was costing me to offer the public
even my book upon dreams—I should have to give away so much
of my own private character in it." He started feeling very sad and
may have remembered the twenty-fourth of July, when the secret
of dreams was revealed to him. He was happy and wrote that he
felt "delighted as the dwarf in the fairy tale because 'the princess
doesn't know.'"[15]

What dwarf, what princess, and what did Louise N. want? What
was she saying when she said she knew, as he was secretly talking
about himself?

What does a woman want? And what does she know?

"The further thoughts which were started up by my conversation with Louise N. went too deep to become conscious. They

were diverted in the direction of the material that had been stirred up in me by the mention of Ridder Haggard's *She*. The judgment 'strangely enough' went back to that book and to another one, *Heart of the World*, by the same author."

Is the heart of the world, the center of the earth, where immortal works are born and emotions never die, the place of which Louise N. may have had some inborn, undue prescience, coming from nobody knows where?

> To know it, you must see it,
> But where and when?

The next day, the old Brücke is there, who makes the trip possible, marks out the space, and shows the way. Freud, who carries deep in his memory the dream of a man with the beak of a bird,[16] sets out to discover the feminine part of himself, in his torn body with the changing landscapes, following guides whose gender is interchangeable, toward the place where the enigma of life becomes clear.

But it is only a dream. Theory is there to summon man back to order and provide him with an inventory of words that temporarily put a stop to his quest. "What we cannot reach flying [like the mother taken away by men with bird beaks] we must reach limping. The Book tells us it is no sin to limp."[17]

Who limps and always drinks water at the fountain? Is it enough to say "you must"? Freud, light-footed dreamer, exhausted watchman dressed in a coat of mail, wakes up in anguish and makes sense of his dream with words, those of Oedipus, law and order.

And that is the way it is. At the very moment where eyes are torn out, where wolves and masks suddenly fly off, the real appears in its extreme concision, more surprising and uncanny than fiction, with its procession of sounds, words, and images like closed lips barred by an index finger.

Notes

Chapter 1

1. I will use the English "phantasy" to translate the French term *fantasme*.—Trans.
2. The word for "stone" is *pierre*.—Trans.
3. Sigmund Freud, "On Narcissism: An Introduction" (1914), *Collected Papers* (New York: Basic Books, 1959), 4: 48; *Gesammelte Werke* (Frankfurt am Main: S. Fischer Verlag, 1952–68), 10: 157; henceforth abbreviated *CP* and *GW*, respectively.—Trans.

Chapter 2

1. Freud, "An Infantile Neurosis" (1918), *CP* 3: 473; *GW* 12: 116.—Trans.
2. Leclaire is evoking the wordplay in "Tu es la femme que j'aime" (You are the woman that I love): *tu es* echoes *tuer* (to kill), *que j'aime* echoes *que j'ai* (that I have), *que* echoes *queue* (tail), and *la femme* echoes *affame* (famish).—Trans.

Chapter 3

1. Johann Wolfgang von Goethe, *The Sorrows of Young Werther* (June 16).
2. Freud, "The Unconscious" (1915), *CP* 4: 119; *GW* 10: 286.—Trans.
3. Freud, "Repression" (1915), *CP* 4: 86; *GW* 10: 250.—Trans.
4. In English, "skin," "corn" or "callus," "body," "gold," and "rose."—Trans.

5. "Philipp' I am thirsty."—Trans.

6. "Foot-head," "rock-sand," "water–to drink."—Trans.

7. "Darling Philippe," "Lili my treasure" or "Lili's treasure," and "beautiful body of Lili," respectively.—Trans.

8. The French translates as follows: *poli,* "polite"; *joli,* "pretty"; *lit,* "bed," and *corps,* "body," or *licorne,* "unicorn."—Trans.

Chapter 4

1. The word for "play," *jeu,* has the same pronunciation as *je* ("I"). —Trans.

2. The word for "game" is *jeu.*—Trans.

3. The word *solitaire* means an "old male boar, living by himself."—Trans.

4. *Père* is French for "father."—Trans.

5. Again, the word for "I" is *je,* for "play" or "game," *jeu.*—Trans.

6. *Moi-je* translates as "me-I."—Trans.

7. This commentary appeared in a notice accompanying the record album *L'Art de la fugue* (Supraphon; Milan Münclinger's version).

8. The word *crever,* slang for "to die," also means "to burst."—Trans.

9. "Vineyards" is the English translation of Leclaire's *la vigne,* Lavigne being the maiden name of Justin's mother.—Trans.

10. The words for "clearing the land" and "deciphering" are *défricher* and *déchiffrer,* respectively.—Trans.

11. Again, "play" is *jeu;* "I," *je.*—Trans.

12. How can one not think of Lucifer (carrier of light), prince of darkness!

Chapter 5

1. Leclaire's "chercheuse" is an unusual feminine form of *chercheur.*—Trans.

2. *La Femme de trente ans* is the title of a novel by Balzac.—Trans.

3. *Supporter* can mean "to stand" in the sense of "to put up with," so this passage could also be translated as "to put up with herself."—Trans.

4. The French *n'être (rien)* means "being (nothing)"; *naître (de rien)* means "to be born (of nothing)."—Trans.

5. The French *sage comme une image* literally means "as well behaved as a picture."—Trans.

6. Freud, *The Interpretation of Dreams* (1900) (New York: Avon Books, 1965), p. 491.—Trans.

7. Freud, *The Origins of Psycho-Analysis* (New York: Basic Books, 1950), letter 134.—Trans.

8. Ibid., letter 107.—Trans.

9. *The Interpretation of Dreams*, p. 491.—Trans.

10. The phrase "clear the land" is a translation of *défricher*; "deciphering" is a translation of *déchiffrer.*—Trans.

11. Freud, "Observations on Transference-Love" (1915) in *Further Recommendations on Technique*, in *The Standard Edition of the Complete Psychological Works*, trans. James Strachey (London: Hogarth Press, 1955–74), 12: 168.—Trans.

12. The French word *impuissance* also means "impotence."—Trans.

13. The French for "taken" is *prise*, for "grip," *prises.*—Trans.

14. "Observations on Transference-Love," *Standard Edition* 12: 162.—Trans.

15. "Primary model" of hysterical dissatisfaction.

16. The word *liquider* also means "to sell cheaply," "to get rid of."—Trans.

17. With "analytic abjection," I follow J.-A. Miller in using one of Lacan's expressions.

18. Jacques Lacan, lecture at the International Convention of Psychiatry, 1950.

Postscript

1. The French term *non-lieu* can also refer to a case dismissed for lack of evidence.—Trans.

2. In Freud, *Contributions to the Psychology of Love* (1918), *CP* 4: 217.—Trans.

3. Arthur Schnitzler, *The Prediction.*—Trans.

4. The emphasis in "*or very rarely happen in fact*" is the author's.—Trans.

5. Freud, "The 'Uncanny'" (1919), *CP* 4: 405.—Trans.

6. Freud, "The Poet and Day-dreaming," *CP* 4: 183.—Trans.

7. Freud, *Letters of Sigmund Freud* (New York: Basic Books, 1960), letter 197.—Trans.

8. "The 'Uncanny,'" *CP* 4: 399.—Trans.

9. Ibid., pp. 399 and 403.—Trans.

10. Ibid., p. 389.—Trans.

11. Renaud's dream, related by Leclaire, uses that same alphabet. The birthmark inscribed in the body and evoked in gestures is as multiple

and diverse in its representations as the paths that lead to it and will never be read. Only from "the meeting of two new voices" can one suspect its closeness.

12. "Double-v" is the name of the letter *w* in French.—Trans.

13. "Das Beste was du wissen kannst— / Darfst du den Buben doch nicht sagen" (Goethe's *Faust*, 1). Freud often quotes these words, spoken by Mephisto to Faust. They go back to one of his childhood memories, one related to a trip he made with his mother from Freiberg to Leipzig, referred to in letter 27 to Fliess. He takes up the quotation again in the associations connected to the dissection dream.

14. *The Interpretation of Dreams*, p. 489.—Trans.

15. *The Origins of Psycho-Analysis*, letter 137.—Trans.

16. *The Interpretation of Dreams*, p. 622. —Trans.

17. Freud ends *Beyond the Pleasure Principle* with these words of the poet Rückert.

Translator's Acknowledgments

I would like to thank all those who encouraged me as I prepared this translation, in particular Terese Lyons, whose revisions to the final manuscript were indispensable, and Jules Fremond, who patiently edited the text as I went along. The ongoing support and interest of my friends, both here and in France, sustained me through the long process, which ranged from being taught to use a computer by Marie-Hélène Estrade or being brought the right dictionary by Foulques de Jouvenel at just the right moment to discussions with Marie-Françoise Bourgin, Frederick Kramer, or Serafina Bathrick. Thanks also to Helen Tartar, at Stanford University Press, for her patience as my deadline receded. The benevolent presence of the author in the background was invaluable, and I grieve that plans to revise the translation with him could not be realized. Finally, I want to thank my husband, Temuri Akhobadze, for his unfailing graciousness throughout long periods of unavailability on my part.

MERIDIAN

Crossing Aesthetics

Library of Congress Cataloging-in-Publication Data

Leclaire, Serge.
    [On tue un enfant. English]
    A child is being killed : on primary narcissism and the death drive /
Serge Leclaire ; translated by Marie-Claude Hays.
        p.   cm. — (Meridian; crossing aesthetics)
    Includes bibliographical references.
    ISBN 0-8047-3140-3 (hardcover : alk. paper). — ISBN 0-8047-3141-1
(pbk. : alk. paper)
    1. Psychoanalysis.   2. Narcissism.   I. Title.   II. Series: Meridian
(Stanford, Calif.)
    BF175.L3913   1998
    150.19'5—dc21   97-23343
                                                                         CIP

∞   This book is printed on acid-free, recycled paper.

Original printing 1998
Last figure below indicates year of this printing:
07   06   05   04   03   02   01   00   99   98